The Twelve Shifts

YOUR SUPERPOWERS FOR
CREATING AN INVINCIBLE LIFE

The Twelve Shifts

YOUR SUPERPOWERS FOR
CREATING AN INVINCIBLE LIFE

Jamil Frazier

Dedication

To my darling Amanda,
thank you for saying no.

Contents

Foreword

We live in a world of easy buttons and elaborate fantasies. This is understandable when considering some of the circumstances in which people find themselves. However, the success we all long to experience does not just manifest, it is intentionally created as we courageously make twelve critical shifts.

With so many voices calling to us to do this or do that, how can we know if this is the answer? How can we know if we can trust this mentor? I always start by asking one question, "Does the mentor have the same teacher?" In other words, no matter how hard it is to hear the mentor's counsel, does it resonate with my soul? Does the mentor have a deep and abiding desire to lift, build, and truly serve and bless others?

When we find one of these mentors we find some very unique characteristics. First and foremost, he or she wants us to discover this journey we are on is "our" hero journey not theirs. He or she wants to awaken our natural gifts, our natural genius, our superpowers.

Second, he or she wants us to know the antagonist—the enemy—is not our circumstances, it is our unhealthy habits of thinking.

Third, he or she willingly and vulnerably shares personal experiences—the dark nights. We discover he or she, too, has broken an ankle or two by stepping in the proverbial potholes of life. As we read, the stories shared inspire us to look deeper into our lives where we find more meaning and purpose and a newfound determination to shift.

Fourth, he or she shares how they learned to dig out and then somehow seem to jump right into our own deep dark hole and show us step-by-step what is required for us to dig out.

The counsel this mentor gives is not always easy to hear. However, it resonates with our soul and we know it is true even if it is hard to hear. As we read, we begin to trust both the messenger and the message. Without hesitation we take that first step and then the next and to our delight, we feel the shift—it's working.

Jamil Frazier is that kind of mentor and The Twelve Shifts is that kind of book. In the book he does not tell you what to do, he shares with you what he did and then invites you to unlock your superpowers and do likewise.

I first heard about Jamil in 2014 from one of his mentors. She said, "You have to meet this leader. He is willing to do whatever it takes to create success. A natural servant leader." I met Jamil in person for the first time in 2015 while doing a retreat in Oregon. Over the years that followed, we have become dear friends. Jamil is the real deal. Born in abject poverty and in circumstances that would emotionally cripple most, Jamil has risen to the highest heights in his profession, while managing to be the consummate husband and father.

When Jamil sent me a pre-release draft of The Twelve Shifts, I consumed it. The minute I finished I sent the following text:

Two words: digestible and brilliant.

This was so Jamil. Honest, daring, vulnerable, committed, compassionate, and crystal clear. They say that those who cannot do, teach. In truth, it is those who have paid the price to figure out the often obscure mysteries of success and who intrinsically love people, as Jamil does, who can't help but teach … and lead.

This book was born out of trial and error, sweat and blood. It is shared so that you can know which shifts are necessary to speed up your journey. My father used to say, "Life is too short to make all the mistakes yourself." Thank God for those who made mistakes, learned great lessons, and then share what they know and do.

Are you ready to surrender any desire for an easy button and trade it in for an awakening of your superpowers? Are you ready to discover the shifts that are required for the success you desire and so richly deserve? Are you willing to follow a mentor whose only mission is your success? If so, it is time to dive head first into The Twelve Shifts!

Foreword

By Kim Fiske

I will never forget the day I received a call from Karen, a good friend and member of my coaching team, asking for help with a potential new team member. "Kim, could you talk to a new coach with me please? He is pretty headstrong."

"Of course," I said.

This was a normal request, as we had frequent calls with new coaches welcoming them to the team, answering any questions they may have about getting started, or adding credibility to the initial mentor (as in Karen's case).

Even though these conversations were common, this one became a special memory. As the call started, I could tell that this man was *not* the most open student! He was on the call to school us about his own plans, how good he was, and to make sure we knew in no uncertain terms who we were talking to. This was my first exposure to Jamil Frazier—and I can tell you, while his confidence still remains, he has become one of the most humble, hungry, and teachable coaches I've ever worked with. And I attribute much of his incredible success to these *shifts*.

That's why reflecting on our first interaction makes me chuckle. The end of that first call was cold. Personally, I didn't expect to see or hear from him again. And for awhile, I was correct. But over the next couple of months, his name was still being mentioned. In fact, I even learned he was begrudgingly coming to our national convention being held in Washington, DC. I thought that was interesting, as this event was across the country from his home in California, and would require him to invest money to attend. I was also curious how he would handle the information he would receive at this event, because the main focus for the company events was transformation, not information.

This event proved to be pivotal in Jamil's personal development journey.

As he became more and more involved in this business, we had more interactions. Slowly, he became humble and coachable. While he didn't resonate with everything all at once, his "true self" was calling to him at a deep level, obviously loud enough to have him stick with this new path.

I'm so glad he did, because it has been such a joy to watch Jamil's journey. What he has accomplished outwardly is only a fraction of what he has allowed himself to endure and learn inwardly. These lessons are far more valuable. The refining process will continue for him, as it does for all of us. I am grateful to be named as a mentor and fellow "consciousness raiser" with him.

I will watch as he leaves his mark on his personal life, and how the ripples will spread to the world, as a result of his influence.

This book is only the start.

Introduction

I sat with an accomplished doctor who had helped thousands of patients through many crises—and now she faced one of her own. But her problem wasn't illness; it was identity. She was considering a career change into my field of health coaching and had asked me for advice. As I listened to her work through intense internal conflict, I asked her if she remembered the story of Jesus calling his disciples. (I knew she would, being a woman of faith, but asked her anyway.) She nodded. I began, "Remember where they were when Jesus found them? They were each working their livelihoods. Some of them were operating the family fishing business, and another was a tax collector."

She nodded again but with a little confusion as to where I was going.

"Do you think any of them imagined what was really in store for them?" I asked. "They each thought they would spend their lives doing something else—and so did their families. But everything changed when they got their calling."

The confusion evaporated, and she saw what I had done.

"If they could change, why can't you?"

WHOM THIS BOOK IS FOR

At its core, that is the message of this book. It is for anyone who has the desire to build something worth leaving behind with their life. Whether it be a church, a family, a business, generational wealth, standards of health, vibrant relationships, or anything in between, this message is about understanding that life can be different, and different can be very good. Different can build a legacy that changes not only your story but the stories of tens of thousands (and beyond).

This book is for the man or woman who is simply looking for more. Who desires more, craves more, and quite frankly, was called to do more, but just can't seem to figure it out. This book is for my thirty-one-year-old self who had done most things "right" up to that point but was still frustrated.

I had all of the building blocks of the good life. I had a great circle of friends. I graduated high school as one of the top running backs in Southern California, so good I received an athletic scholarship to college to play football. I didn't do drugs or consume excess alcohol—in fact, I'm still a lightweight when it comes to drinking. I grew up in church. I went to a Christian private college where, on top of undergraduate studies, I had to complete a boatload of theology courses and attend chapel at least three times per week.

I married a girl so beautiful that if you walked by her right now, you'd stop dead in your tracks, arrested by her physical beauty; then, when you actually got the chance to know her, you'd freeze again because she is a goddess who is also down to earth, genuine, and loving. I was a pharmaceutical sales representative for a division of one of the largest companies in U.S. history, Johnson & Johnson. I had a company car and an expense account. I had worked my way into a six-figure income.

I had the tiger by the tail. From the outside, the American Dream was my reality. But on the inside, it was a different story. All of the accolades, awards, and Instagram highlights were a facade. For all of my success, I was still broke financially, mentally, physically, emotionally, relationally, spiritually—and all the other -lys. Today, the more people I meet and work with, the more I hear this same story just with different actors.

How is it that so many of us are following what we know as the "blueprint" of life and success but are still as jacked up as I was trying to figure out how to do better? Fighting daily just to be happy?

As I share my stories and the pivotal lessons I've learned along the way, my burning desire and deepest prayer is that if the scenarios I just described sound at all like you, that you will find a unique breakthrough on your own path toward excellence and transformation. And that you will do so by having mental shifts of your own.

SORRY, KIDS, SANTA ISN'T REAL

Why the *Twelve Shifts*? In fact, what is a shift? To be honest I had twenty-seven *huge* shifts over the past six years, but if I outlined all of them, this book would be three thousand pages, and I doubt anyone would read it because it wouldn't even fit in a carry-on bag! So, I chose the twelve most important. Each shift is a major mindset transformation that produced tremendous growth in every area of my life. What happens between our ears has the power to change everything in our lives, for better or worse.

These shifts started once I decided to quit my full-time job in medical sales to pursue a home-based business as a certified health coach (as my doctor friend was considering). I was nervous but decided to risk it all. I took the leap from what I saw as the "safety" of a corporate job into unknown territory as the master of my own fate. And, as you'll see, each shift dismantled truths I had absolutely *known* were true for the previous thirty-one years.

Only, I had been wrong. The world didn't work the way I thought it did. Every shift was a tectonic move that radically changed my entire landscape. Most were jarring. After all, how can something be true and all of a sudden not be true? Good question.

If you live in the United States, chances are you (or people around you) believed in Santa Claus as a child. If you lived in a family who celebrated Christmas, from the time you were a baby, your family likely had a ritual, and perhaps it looked something like this: Your family draped your house in Christmas lights, then visited the same lot as the previous year to buy a Christmas tree. The family dressed up in silly clothing embroidered with reindeer and green-hatted elves, all so Mom and Dad could take pictures of you and your siblings that you didn't want any part of. You lashed the tree on top of the car and raced home to carefully place all the ornaments one by one. Meanwhile, your siblings fought over who Dad would lift up on his big, broad shoulders to complete the experience by placing that shining star high on top of the tree. This, of course, signified that Christmas, and Santa Claus himself, were indeed close.

For the next three weeks, you knew that, come Christmas Eve, the jolly man would jump in his sleigh powered by a formidable team of reindeer and show up right on time to take a bite out of the chocolate cookie Mom had left on the table, washing it down with the glass of milk. (If you lived in Southern California, low-fat; whole milk if you lived in Georgia.) All while illegally trespassing, which was perfectly okay, because Santa would complete his duty of leaving you and your siblings a hearty stash of glistening gifts. Somehow, he knew that you wanted the little green army men, and that your sisters wanted all the Little Mommy Goodnight Snuggles Baby Dolls.

Do you remember those days? For many kids, they were perfect, jovial, blissful. What if someone had told you that Santa, in fact, did not exist, that not only was he made up, but that all the songs about Rudolph's red nose, the doting Mrs. Claus, him sliding down the chimney, his bites out of your mama's cookies, and the twelve days of Christmas … all of it … was just a dream? That it was all a figment of society's warped imagination?

As a kid, you might have said, "There's absolutely no way! Of course Santa is real."

Then something happened. You got older and learned a little bit more. You were exposed to new ways of thinking. You heard different philosophies. You started questioning your own belief systems. You became conscious of the wider world.

You experienced SHIFTS.

All of a sudden, the very thing that you had known with absolute certainty for YEARS to be true, you realized was a lie. You shifted into a new reality, a new stream of consciousness, a new level of awareness. You had an awakening. And as ancient scriptures describe it, you were "born again."

Or how about this one: If you were a child of the '80s like me, you grew up with some classic scary movies. *Nightmare on Elm Street, Friday the 13th, Child's Play*, and that one creepy movie with those clowns who went around killing everyone after dark. As a kid, do you remember feeling doomed the very moment you wandered outside after sunset? Death was imminent. The Grim Reaper himself was waiting around every corner, sickle in hand, ready to strike. And God forbid there be a full moon. That was even more evidence that Jason was waiting for you to leave your house, only for you to sprint away while he slowly stalked you, inevitably catching up and slashing you to bits.

Remember those days? Maybe I had an overactive imagination. But for me, darkness and nighttime were synonymous with death and destruction. Then, as you grew older, these midnight villains faded into childhood fairytales along with Santa Claus and his friendly helpers at the North Pole. You had a simple awakening, a shift. You realized that what was once real for you wasn't actually true. At that moment you saw the world differently. You learned, at least in part, that the fears we run from are more than untrue; they don't serve us.

I've learned that, much like the stories of Santa Claus, Freddy Krueger, Jason, Chucky, the weird clowns, and all of their beautiful, magical, made-up mess of lies, is exactly how many of our lives play out. Unfounded promises and untrue fears dominate our lives—until we have the life-changing shifts I share in the pages ahead. Some of them are gradual, like a slow sunrise revealing an incredible landscape before you. Others are like an atomic bomb of clarity. In an instant you see how the obstacles have been pushed aside. The storm subsides, replaced by bright, cheery sunshine.

That is called a *shift*, my friend.

HOW THE TWELVE SHIFTS WILL HELP YOU

Why twelve? Why not six, ten, or fourteen? The truth is that there's something about the number twelve that has always stuck with me. It's called to me since I was a little boy. While doing research for this book, I realized the number twelve has long been considered divine by people of various cultures throughout the ages. You see, twelve represents completion, harmony, motivation, and achievement.

- *There were twelve tribes in Israel …*
- *There were twelve Olympians as the Greek gods of the pantheon …*

- *There are twelve petals in the Hindu Anahata (the heart chakra) …*
- *There are twelve days of Christmas …*
- *There are twelve months in a year …*

Twelve is at the very end of the numerology spectrum, and it offers those who see it in their daily life the opportunity to turn over a new leaf by offering chances to close certain life stages and move into bigger and better things. Twelve is like a curtain call, inviting you to get your affairs in order so you can benefit from the windfall that God is about to bestow on you. My intention is to help you, my reader, do just that.

It's time to turn over new leaves by uncovering deep truths. It's time to shift our minds to change our lives. You see, when our mindsets change, so does everything else. The transformation of our thoughts revolutionizes our lives.

So, I offer twelve different mindset shifts that you will need to make in order to bring about the transformation and success you desire in your life. These mindset shifts will help you understand that you don't know what you don't know, and that's okay—it's not your fault. But while it's not your fault, it is your responsibility to undo the damage and make the changes that you want in your life and business.

Best of all, you will uncover superpowers you never knew you had. Superpowers to create a formidable, unstoppable life. Superpowers to build a life so much bigger than you ever thought possible. And just like Superman, Spiderman, Batman, and the rest of our canon of superheroes, these powers are intended for the benefit of everyone around you—from your family to your city to society as a whole. All you need to do is realize you're wearing Clark Kent's glasses, so you can take them off and see how different life can really be.

To help you do this, you will also find forty *Mental Mentors* strategically placed throughout the book. These are a collection of the most powerful lessons, sayings, and thoughts from the many mentors I've had in my life. They are responsible for helping me elevate my mindset from poverty to abundance and making many of the shifts I will share. From ancient Roman emperors to the first business leaders who believed in me, some of the wisdom echoes from ancient halls or was whispered by modern lips. All of their counsel, however, holds golden keys to unlock our minds and experience what is truly possible.

Are you ready? Let's go.

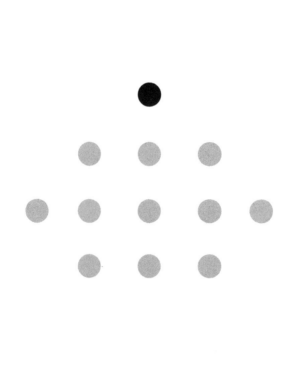

You Have Superpowers

*"If you change the way you look at things,
the things you look at change."*

– DR. WAYNE DYER

There's something hiding inside of you that I'll bet you didn't even know was there.

It's soft but hard. It attracts love and sows hate. It brings riches and leaves destruction. It turns wise men into fools and transforms great empires into specks of dust.

Know what it is? You're about to find out.

Back in the 1950s, in a Buddhist monastery tucked away in the jungles of Burma, an ancient statue needed to be relocated to make room for a new highway. The monks agreed to the move and began to make arrangements, taking special care to plan for the relocation of the priceless relic, a 10-foot-tall clay statue of Buddha.

On moving day, a crane arrived, and the monks began to carefully secure the statue within a series of straps and harnesses. But as the machine began to lift the statue, something unexpected happened—the crane began to creak and groan, its engine straining as though it were trying to hoist an entire mountainside. The statue was far heavier than anyone could have anticipated.

Worse, the ancient Buddha had begun to crack. Fault lines ripped across its clay surface, and both the monks and the moving crew rushed toward the statue as the crane released its grip. They began to realize that more delicate equipment would be needed to complete the move.

That night, to further complicate the situation, it began to rain. Once again, the monks rushed forward to save their clay Buddha, covering the statue with tarps to shield it from further damage.

It was then, in the dead of night, that the head monk struck out into the storm to check on the statue and his monks' attempts to protect it. When he arrived, flashlight in hand, another strange thing happened— beneath the cracks in the statue, a golden light had begun to glow.

Wide-eyed, the head monk rushed back into the monastery, and, returning with a hammer and chisel, began to furiously chip away at the statue, ignoring the cries of protest from the monks around him.

Each blow of the hammer and chisel removed another chunk of clay from the statue, revealing a solid gold interior beneath.

The monks fell back in awe as he worked, realizing they were in the presence of something truly majestic and truly transformative. For decades, they had passed by the statue, thinking it a simple clay carving—when in fact it was a secret treasure waiting to be discovered.

Historians today believe that the golden Buddha statue had been covered with clay by Thai monks several hundred years earlier to protect it from an attack by the Burmese army. The monks were all killed in the attack, and the cover-up was so good it lasted for centuries.

CHILDREN OF CLAY

I love to tell people the story of the clay statue. Not just because it's an amazing story, but because the reaction people have to it is *tangible* and *real*. I love watching their jaws drop, their eyes shine. I love it when understanding clicks, when my audience realizes that they are more than they seem, even to themselves. I love to see the question form in their minds: "What if I'm made of gold inside too?"

And, more importantly: "What sort of clay is covering *me* up?"

The Thai monks in the story above wanted to hide their precious golden statue of Buddha in order to protect it.

In the same way, we often resort to hiding to protect ourselves from the cruelty, danger, and judgment of the world. We throw clay—figuratively speaking—onto ourselves to keep us safe, hidden, and trouble-free. The problem is that our brains often create problems that aren't based in reality or factual in any way.

We often think and act from a place of clay—from a false exterior we've been forced to develop over the years, or even chosen to develop in response to our circumstances. Up until I was thirty-two years old, I, too, was operating from this place. I spent the majority of my life viewing myself as a victim, as *less than*, as a man of clay through and through.

But what if I'm not a man of clay? What if I'm a man of gold—or even a man of steel?

And what if you are too?

What happens when we slough off the clay and begin to think and act like the incredible golden beings we truly are underneath?

CLAY LIES AND GOLDEN TRUTHS

Seven years ago, I began chiseling away at my own husk of clay. It was incredibly difficult—the clay had hardened around my mind and body early on, during my childhood, and I had gotten used to it. In a way, I had grown to accept and even love it. It had become a part of me as it becomes a part of all of us.

From the time we are children, our culture covers up our gold with dirt, muck, mire, limitations, limiting beliefs, faulty philosophies, the sense of being *less than*, and all other manner of clay. Through no fault of our own, we are conditioned to view ourselves as much less valuable than we truly are.

For years, we are told:

- *"Don't sit there."*
- *"Don't be too worldly."*
- *"You're the shy one in the family."*
- *"Don't stand out."*
- *"Don't make noise."*
- *"You can't ask for that."*
- *"That's not for someone like you."*
- *"Don't talk to adults like that."*
- *"Wait your turn."*
- *"Don't associate with* those *people."*
- *"The apple doesn't fall far from the tree."*
- *... and, of course, continue to fill in the blanks from your own experience.*

We are programmed by statements like these—limiting statements that do not allow us to grow past the period at the end. We internalize the beliefs, act on them, and begin to actually believe them. We treat these false statements as unquestionable truths.

When I was little, I learned that since my family had weight issues, I, too, was destined to have weight issues. I was told my spelling was poor, and I had speech issues. My destiny was predetermined by bad genetics. "Our family is big-boned," they told me, "and that's it." There was nothing to be done about it. We were a family of big bones and small calves. Of poor spelling and slow speech.

I don't believe our society, school systems, and families are conditioning us like this on purpose—or rather, I don't believe their intent is to hurt us or to keep us down. Rather, those doing the conditioning believe they are doing us a favor, protecting us by telling us "how it is," by offering us tough love, and by tempering our dreams so that we will be less hurt if (and when) they come crashing down. It's just like the Burmese monks who originally covered the golden Buddha statue in clay to protect it from the big scary world. And I can appreciate that.

But despite their good intentions, those monks were covering something beautiful with a bunch of muck, mire, dirt, clay, and (if you'll excuse my French) a whole bunch of shit. They were smothering it, dimming the statue's golden glow and diminishing its power and worth.

Which is why it is so crucial that we chisel away our own clay coverings and reveal our own true selves beneath. As Paulo Coelho said, "Maybe the journey isn't so much about becoming anything. Maybe the journey is about unbecoming everything that isn't really you, so you can be who you were meant to be in the first place."

In my case, there was a *lot* of clay to chip away. In fact, I didn't know how much clay there *was* until I began to chip away at it. And the same will probably be true for you.

But even though the process was long and difficult, I kept on, always searching for the glint of gold beneath. Each blow of my hammer exposed another layer of lies, another layer of false identity, another layer of mediocrity and excuses and illusory protection.

And the same can happen for you, piece by piece and layer by layer. The process happens over thousands of incremental changes, powered by the twelve major mindset shifts outlined in this book.

They said, "You cannot inspire people to follow your lack of commitment. People will ONLY follow what they admire."

— THINK LIFE *is* DIFFERENT

Together, we are going to explore the major renovations, revelations, and resets that I have used to transform my life. And I invite you to do the same.

EVERY SUPERHERO HAS AN ORIGIN

When I was a kid, I loved comic books and superhero movies. I wasn't particular about which ones. Heck, I even thought the elementary school rage of *My Little Pony* was cool. (Seriously—if you're unfamiliar with the show, it's about a band of magical, flying horses who save the world twenty minutes at a time. It's fantastic.)

The size, shape, gender, and species of hero didn't matter to me—my friends and I ate it all up regardless. What *mattered* was the amazing powers these heroes held deep inside of them … and what they *did* with them.

One byproduct of the twelve mindset shifts I've made over the last several years has been the realization that we all have amazing powers deep inside of us as well. Each and every single one of us has superpowers. This is not a joke.

The problem is, many of us don't know they're there. Because, for the majority of us, these superpowers—the solid gold gleam within us all, our true selves—are covered up by clay. But once we find the courage to start chipping it away, those powers begin to shine through. We become more than we were told we ever could be. We become the superheroes of our own lives—and even the lives of others.

If you know anything about comics, you'll know that every superhero has an origin story. In fact, many superheroes begin as normal, inconsequential people, that is, people covered in metaphorical clay.

It isn't until the need to realize their strength arises that they are able to begin growing into their full potential.

This need for strength generally arises from an obstacle or a place of pain, ironically, the very thing or things the clay is trying to protect us from. Many people never have the courage to sacrifice the protection and face the pain. But it is by facing painful pasts that superheroes engineer their formidable futures. So, we need to be willing to confront and overcome the pain that may come when we begin to chisel away the clay.

And the day you begin to chip away at the clay—the day you begin to expose the painful layer of lies and *shit* that's been covering you up—is the day your origin story begins.

For instance, Batman's parents are murdered by a criminal when he's just a boy, a painful moment that propels him into a career of crimefighting. It's not an easy transition for him, but he does it anyway.

Superman is forced to leave his home-world as a child, and after being taken in by a loving human couple, feels the moral imperative to use his alien powers to protect other humans. Again, he initially struggles against this identity shift, but at the end of the day reveals the gold (or in his case, the steel) beneath.

Spider-Man is an orphaned kid forced to witness the murder of his uncle before stepping fully into his destiny. And again, it's not easy. He's young and vulnerable, and his enemies are massive and powerful. But he does it anyway.

We need to do it anyway too. You will never grow into your formidable self by hiding behind and refusing to confront a painful past. For me, the battle was divorce, potential separation from my son, and watching everyone else around me succeed—leaving me far behind.

I had to do the very same thing I'm telling you to do. It was unbelievably hard. But I did it anyway. And it was unbelievably *worth it*. Just like Batman, Superman, and Spider-Man, I had to confront issues related to my parents and guardians in order to step up into my true superpowers. And you can do it too.

KICKING THE CURB

Today, I truly believe my father did the best he could with what he had to work with.

This wasn't always the case, but with age and children of my own came reflective wisdom, and I am grateful that I am able to look back on him now with empathy, forgiveness, and love.

My father spent my early childhood years bouncing in and out of prison. When I was five, he went to prison for a longer stint—in fact,

I don't remember him returning home until I was around eleven—and it had a major impact on both of our lives.

When he was released from prison, my father moved back home with us. He had gotten my mother pregnant just before his arrest years earlier and had never met my little sister—his daughter. But despite our joy at his homecoming, and our need to love him and be loved by him, for reasons I did not understand back then, our family was somehow *not enough* for him. His stay in our home was short, and he soon moved out and found a new family.

Weekend after weekend, my father promised to come pick me up so we could spend time together. And every time he made a promise like this, my heart soared with hope. But he rarely showed up. Instead, he left me kicking the curb, waiting around for a man I desperately wanted to see, cursing myself for trusting his promises.

It was in these moments that I allowed his clay to gather on me. Little by little, layer by layer, consciously or unconsciously, I let the feelings of being *unwanted*, of being *not enough*, of being *foolish* enough to believe his empty words, build up and begin to obscure my golden core of power and truth.

And little by little, I began to forget the innate childhood knowledge that I was made perfect, forged of solid gold without flaw.

This is when I began to develop the clay husks of scarcity, bitterness, and a destructive mindset. This is when I developed a hardness, a protective layer, in response to the hurt. This was when I began to distrust authority figures. This was my clay.

And for over thirty years, this way of thinking robbed me of solid relationships, career advancements, business endeavors, and overall happiness. In protecting myself from my father, I also pushed away my teachers, my high school and college football coaches, potential mentors, and every other authority figure along the way.

It became my natural inclination to continue to protect myself in all the wrong ways, to shift blame to others, act like a victim, and compensate for feeling *not enough* with anger, ego, and a massive chip on my shoulder.

They said, "You cannot take more withdrawals out of life than you've deposited. Thinking you can do so will be frustrating and delusional."

— THINK LIFE *is* DIFFERENT

Clay is applied in sticky layers that hardens over the years, and it's interesting (or, more accurately, horrifying) to observe in retrospect what we allow it to do to us. But no matter how much clay is layered upon us, that solid gold core of power *never goes away*.

The gold is still under there, waiting to be revealed by a hammer and chisel—the hard and often painful work that comes with engineering your own origin story.

"Y'ALL AREN'T GOING TO SIT AROUND AND *USE* ME!"

Even without my father in the picture, our house was pretty chaotic as I was growing up. It seemed as though people were constantly coming and going, a steady stream of new faces flowing in and out of our lives.

My mother is, to this day, one of those women who can carry the entire world on her back and make it look easy. She was a single mother throughout my childhood, and I honestly don't know how she did it, outside of a ton of hard work, massive overexertion, and maybe a couple of miracles.

But while her actions were incredibly selfless, she had this funny habit where she would *always* make sure you knew *just how much* she was sacrificing for you. It wasn't malicious, and maybe it wasn't even intentional. But it was there.

It came out in this catchphrase: "Y'all aren't just going to sit around and *use* me!" I heard her say it hundreds of times throughout my childhood, and, like so much other clay, it stuck. And to it stuck lessons that sacrifice wasn't free, everyone needed to chip in equally, and injustice needed to be called out.

Now, these aren't necessarily negative lessons and values. *But*, when ingrained in my clay and allowed to fester, they became insidious and even dangerous beliefs. No one was going to *use* me. No one was going to get a free ride off of my hard work. Only I could profit from my success.

These beliefs became increasingly detrimental to my overall happiness and success, but they didn't explode until decades later … in my marriage.

I cannot remember a time in my life where being successful was not a primary ambition. My earliest memories are filled with a desire to be "rich" (… whatever *that* is). I desperately wanted to have nice things, and even at a young age, I clearly remember my drive to accomplish everything I possibly could in life. I wanted to *be* somebody. I wanted to rise above the average and the normal, so much so that "normal" felt like a disease to me.

But my wife, Amanda, did not share my ambitions and aspirations. She didn't feel the need or the drive to match the salary I was making at the time from my pharmaceutical sales job. Amanda felt … "normal." And "normal" felt like a disease that I was in danger of contracting every day.

Of course, today I realize that Amanda had her own unique gifts and strengths; they simply didn't manifest the same way that mine did. And as with my father, I didn't realize the truths that she was conveying to me until years later. Today, I fully realize and appreciate all of her strengths.

But at the time, perception was reality. And my perception was that while *I* cared about working hard to earn the trappings of worldly success, Amanda did *not*. Through the lens of my mother's clay and my own festering beliefs, all I saw was a woman with no ambition of her own, who fully intended to ride my coattails to success. Through the lens of my mother's clay, all I saw was a woman who was pulling me with her into the quicksand, keeping me down—two steps forward, three steps back.

In short, I saw a woman who was *using me*. And that could not stand.

In psychology, there is a phenomenon called "confirmation bias." Basically, it means that we only see evidence that backs up what we are *already* inclined to believe, and, subconsciously, we ignore anything and everything to the contrary. Every day, we see more and more signals that justify our bias and solidify our belief.

Every day, I catalogued more evidence of what I already (mistakenly) believed about my wife and her perceived shortcomings. I was unconsciously building a case against her in the role of self-righteous judge, jury, and figurative executioner. I believed her to be wrong, just as I believed myself to be right.

Now, what we believe becomes our reality, even if what we believe is distorted beyond reason. And inevitably, we begin to live into these distorted realities, leaning into them with an unrelenting pressure until they become our truth.

Until they lead us down a path of destruction.

From the outside, my path didn't necessarily *look* destructive—in fact, it appeared to be positive, constructive, and downright empowering. In the summer of 2012, I decided to leave my safe, secure, and high-earning corporate job as a pharmaceutical salesman to start a health coaching business.

It looks and sounds admirable, right? But the problem was, I didn't leave that job because the man was keeping me down. I didn't leave because I felt exploited by the big, bad corporate pharmaceutical monster. No.

I left out of pure and poisonous ego. I left out of spite.

I left because *I felt like my wife was using me.*

I left because I had something to prove. I left because I *refused* to be the martyr, because I refused to accept a marriage in which I perceived that I was the only hardworking partner, because "Y'all aren't just going to sit around and *use* me!"

Of course, my perception of Amanda was not true. It wasn't even *close* to being true. Amanda was a behaviorist who worked with children. She was living wholly into her truth and her values, and just because she wasn't making the same amount of money that *I* was did not mean she wasn't using her life to do good and serve others.

But my untrue beliefs had become my reality, and it was from that untrue reality that I took action.

Needless to say, leaving my job out of a place of spite and ego did not go over very well. True to Newton's third law, for every action, there is an equal and opposite reaction. Because of this, I caused our marriage to be impacted by the same negative force that I had been giving off over the past several years, in the very worst way.

HER OWN CLAY

As time went on, I invested myself more and more in my health coaching business, and I tried to convince Amanda to leave her own job and join me. But for reasons I did not understand at the time, she wasn't having it.

"I don't like to sell," she would tell me. Or, "I'm not a salesperson."

"But you'd be so good at this," I would counter. "Why don't you join me?"

"All you do is *sell* people on getting involved with the company," was her swift response, and I noticed that the word *sell* was dripping with disdain.

This conversation continued off and on down the same road for years, always ending with this impasse, this disdain of *selling*. Finally, after two years, I dropped it and stopped trying to convince her to join me.

Then one day, on a whim, Amanda joined me for one of my seminars ... and something clicked. Or, in the context of this book, her mindset made a *shift*.

"Oh, my goodness," she said afterward, "so this is what you do? This is *exactly* what I do as a behaviorist! You just do it with adults, while I do it with kids!"

I nodded and agreed, happy about this shift in her thinking, and a short time later, I mustered up the courage to ask her why she was so aggressively opposed to sales and selling.

Amanda sat and thought about it for a few minutes before replying, and what she revealed was fascinating: "I think it's because when I was a little girl, my sisters and I would be home with my mother when tele-marketers called. I remember her getting so angry that she hung up the phone in frustration at '*those salespeople.*' She complained that all they did was bug people, trying to *force* them into buying things they didn't need."

Amanda paused and considered. "I guess that experience left a bad taste in my mouth for sales."

This, my friends, is clay.

For nearly thirty years, Amanda had believed that salespeople were *bad people* who forced their services and wares onto unsuspecting victims. She believed that selling was inherently manipulative, and that *being sold to* was a type of violence to get angry at and fight against. She had no logical reason to believe these things, other than her mother's reaction. But for nearly thirty years, she had believed thoughts that were not even originally hers. They had been given to her by her mother, presented as truth, and of course, as a child, she had believed them.

And held on to them.

It made me wonder: what had she been thinking about *me* this whole time in my role as a salesperson? Did she see me as a manipulator, as someone who preyed upon hapless victims? Did she have the same self-righteous thoughts about me as I did about her?

For me, the act of sales is more about listening, empathy, asking questions to understand, and making a person's life better. And for Amanda, it was one of the worst things a person could do and be.

It still makes me wonder—at any given time, whose thoughts are we thinking? Whose thoughts had Amanda been thinking throughout our marriage? And whose thoughts had *I* been thinking, for that matter? How were those thoughts serving our family? And worse, how had they been robbing us of true communication, love, and joy?

The nature of clay is that we are covered in it and yet blind to it until that first shift in our thinking. It took me years to recognize how much clay was clinging to me and even longer to begin chipping it away.

And all the while, it controlled my thinking and my behavior—just as it did for Amanda. Just as it is doing for you.

So, I ask you: whose thoughts are you thinking?

What actions do you take every day because of those thoughts?

Have you forgotten that underneath all of that clay, you are a flawless and beautiful being who can do, as ancient scriptures tell us, "all things?"

What will it take for you to see the clay that covers you?

And what will it take for you to begin to reveal the golden treasure—your true self, your superpowers—beneath?

MENTORS AND GUIDES

All of the greatest stories about heroes feature a mentor or guide. Batman had Alfred. Luke Skywalker had Yoda. Frodo was extremely lucky and had both Gandalf *and* Sam.

These mentors and guides are the experienced (and often unassuming) sages who have been through it before, who have recognized their own clay and begun to chisel it away. These guides provide wisdom to the heroes when they need it most and also tend to be the ones to initially point out the hero's own thick layer of clay.

This is incredibly helpful and necessary, because as I stated above: *we tend to be blind to our own clay.* We need someone to point it out so that we can begin to remove it and move past it.

In early 2012, I began to work with a new business mentor named Karen. She possessed the uncanny ability to ask me tough questions that smacked me upside the head—all wrapped up in grace, humility, and a shining Colgate smile. She was the very first person in my life to point out the fact that I was covered in clay.

I thought of Karen's uncanny questions as Jedi mind tricks, since they often left me dazed and thinking, "What just happened? Did I just get verbally beat down or verbally hugged? Or both?" This amazing individual was somehow able to point out my clay while reminding me of my inner gold. It was the best thing that could possibly have happened to me at that time in my life.

As Karen continued to mentor, support, train, and believe in me, I realized that she had become my rock. I realized just how impossible the task of seeing my clay would be without her.

Even though I had already been trying my best to believe in myself, she became my sure footing to do so. Even though I was already ambitious, I strove even harder to make her proud. Praise from Karen became an addiction ... and I was constantly seeking my next fix.

Naturally —inevitably—after a couple of months, Karen began to attract other young rock stars to mentor, support, and train. And immediately, I felt *threatened*. How dare she give away my drugs to someone else? Who was she to share her Jedi mind tricks with other padawans? Why would she abandon me after everything we had been through together, after everything we had accomplished? Where was her loyalty? Why wouldn't she *keep her word* and *work with me and only me*?

Of course, Karen had never promised to work with *me and only me*. Her words were not solely *my* drugs. They were not drugs at all. She did not belong to me, and I did not have any right to think of her as my possession. She did not *owe* me her loyalty or even her mentorship. Even as I write this, it sounds incredibly ridiculous that I would have had such thoughts.

But, since I'm being honest, that was what it *felt* like. That was my perception. And my perception was my reality.

My reaction of feeling angry, threatened, and afraid was reminiscent of my college football days. In those days I had been a top player, and yet every year the coaches would recruit the next young hotshot to replace me ... and take what I had identified as my birthright. How dare they replace me, I remember thinking, when I had given them so much? Who were they to give their praise of me to someone else, someone *new*?

As Karen spent more and more time with the other Jedi-in-training, I grew increasingly dissatisfied. And just as I had done with Amanda, I began to indulge my confirmation bias and gather what I perceived as evidence that *she didn't care*. Around every corner was proof that she was no longer there for me, that she had moved on. That she had *betrayed* me.

From where I stood, it was all about *me*. I saw that I was no longer important to her, and she was throwing it in my face. She posted pictures of herself on social media with my rival understudies just to spite me. She sent flowers to the other Jedi trainees, who would then post pictures of them to make me jealous. She traveled across state lines to visit the others but couldn't drive just a couple miles to meet me.

Every day, mired in my mindset of self-serving fear, anger, jealousy, and suspicion, I gathered more evidence of Karen's abandonment and treachery. I convinced myself that I was right—she had moved on, and I was left kicking the curb, waiting around for yet another authority figure who would never show up. I was little Jamil all over again, waiting for a father who would never return.

Yikes. Talk about clay.

While my feelings *felt* true, my assumptions about Karen were obviously not. She had not abandoned me. She was a professional. She was not doing anything out of spite, and she was not purposefully making me jealous. That was all me—*my* clay and *my* ego.

And in a way, it was all about me. It was *my* anger, pain, insecurity, and fear telling stories to serve a mind that had forgotten about the solid-gold statue inside of myself. It was my confirmation bias indicating that I did not deserve to have someone care about and invest in me. It was my disbelief in my own self-worth, which led to scarcity, bitterness, and a destructive mindset.

The bad news is that, when we look for evidence to support our own false beliefs and assumptions, we usually find it. As Dr. Wayne Dyer said, "When you change the way you look at things, the things you look at change."

But the good news is when we put aside our short-sighted focus on our own clay and begin to earnestly search for truth, we can find that too.

A good mentor can help you with this process. In the end, I went back to Karen, explained my findings to her, and admitted that she was right—and that I had a lot that I wanted to work on. In turn, Karen continued to work with me, coaching me into setting aside my damaging fears, false perceptions, and toxic ego. She helped me begin to see the husk of clay that had covered me—and gave me the support and encouragement I needed to begin to chisel it away. Today, she remains

They said, "If you want things to change for you, it's easy: you'll have to change."

— THINK LIFE *is* DIFFERENT

my foremost mentor and good friend, and continues to ask hard questions and give great life advice.

In working with Karen, I learned how to leave my ego, pride, and arrogance behind to become coachable. Despite my own health coaching business and expertise, I began to realize the value in coaching for myself, *by* myself. I started spending more time speaking to myself than anyone else (often out loud, which made a lot of people think I was crazy). In doing so, I realized my thoughts weren't serving me as well as I'd thought. I realized I had been coated in a *lot* of clay and that it was not just affecting me but others around me. I realized what it meant to acknowledge that the clay was there, and what it meant to begin to scrape it away.

I began to understand that I had control over my own mindset, how I saw and interpreted the world around me. Surprisingly few people understand this, and breaking through into this way of thinking is how we begin to shatter the clay that has hardened around us.

Asking, "Is this thought serving me?" is a great first step into the world of gold. It's the first step *out* of the clay. It is then that we realize we can ask this question at any time, evaluate our mindsets at any time, and thus create new and improved stories for ourselves at any time.

Just like Dr. Wayne Dyer promised, my shift in mindset was followed by a shift in environment, and I finally began to take control and associate myself with people who thought on a higher plane than I did. I was no longer taking on others' clay, but rather reflecting others' gold. (We'll talk about this more in-depth later in this book, in Shift Nine.)

But most importantly, just like so many heroes in so many stories, I had finally begun to realize that my power—my precious, solid-gold statue—had been inside of me all along.

THE SHIFT TO GOLD

We are imperfect beings of both gold and clay. And even when we begin to chisel away the clay, there is no guarantee that we will be able to scrape 100 percent of it away. But realizing it is there, and realizing that it is driving many of the thoughts and actions that keep us from true growth and success, is the very first step. The very first shift.

However, we cannot focus entirely on the clay. We also need to realize that there is gold within us. We need to realize that *we have superpowers*, and that those superpowers are rooted in the gold. We need to understand that within the gold is our own potential for *real and lasting change*.

We will get to what it means to realize and live into our superpowers in the next several chapters of this book. For where we are *right now* in our journey, it is enough to realize that both elements are there within us—the gold *and* the clay—and that we have the power to ask which one is serving us at any given time.

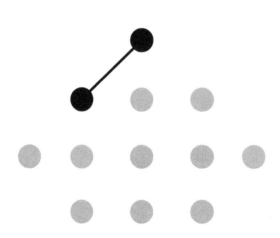

Shift Two

Do Your Own Push-ups

> *"You have to take responsibility*
> *for your own life."*
>
> – OPRAH WINFREY

Growing up in my neighborhood in Pasadena, California, to be superhuman meant one thing: getting an athletic scholarship. All the little Black boys strove to attain this highest height of success. We didn't have many friends whose goal was to graduate valedictorian or make the dean's list. Instead, it was all about becoming an unstoppable athlete. If you did this, you would become Moses, the promised one who would lead your neighborhood out of the desert of obscurity.

All of the other boys who looked like me wanted a football scholarship, and, in the fifth grade, that's exactly what I wanted too. However, as I grew older, it became clear that my sport was baseball. I was a natural and practiced at it more than all other sports combined. When eighth grade rolled around, I set my sights on becoming the best hitter not just in my city but in my entire region.

That meant going head-to-head with thousands of talented athletes, and I was more than up to the challenge. Because when you have a goal that big, you have to take equal action. Trying to be the biggest fish in a big pond requires more than natural talent—it means putting in the work. *Serious* work.

So that's what I did.

1,095,000 SWINGS

Without any adult ever asking me to, I dove headfirst into a rhythm of intense practice. For two years, my daily schedule looked like this:

1. *Go to school and dream about baseball.*

2. *Come home, head back to my bedroom, and trade my backpack for a bat.*

3. *Take five hundred swings with my left hand and then switch stances.*

4. *Take five hundred swings with my right hand and change positions.*

5. *Take five hundred full swings, envisioning a home run every time.*

6. *Go prone and pump out one hundred push-ups.*

7. *Roll over and crush three hundred crunches.*

8. *Let a big smile light up my sweaty face.*

After two years of doing this, my swing was dialed in. I'd had more RBIs and grand slams in my bedroom than any pro in history.

Now, why on earth would an eighth-grade boy put in this much work on his own? I didn't have a coach making me do it. My mom wasn't on my case for me to get my swings in. It was just me, my bat, and my drive to be the best.

Somehow, I knew that if I was going to dominate my region and be a great baseball player, no one was going to do it for me. Nobody else could jump into my body and do the 73,000 push-ups, the 219,000 sit-ups, or the 1,095,000 swings of the bat *for* me during those two years. My athletic performance was tied to my effort and *my effort alone*.

Oddly enough, even though I innately understood how this principle applied to athletics, I failed to understand it anywhere else. I failed to take responsibility for my own growth in other areas, a personal failing that chased me into adulthood.

"IT'S NOT MY FAULT!"

In the absence of personal responsibility comes a vacuum that is most often filled with blame. It feels better and easier when something isn't our fault, when something isn't our responsibility to fix. Blame is easy. Responsibility is hard. And we tend to gravitate toward the *easy*, because why would anyone willingly choose the difficult path?

In academics, I blamed my teachers for my poor grades. I believed that I wasn't getting the help I needed, so … guess what? All of those bad grades weren't my fault! It wasn't *my* responsibility to learn. It was *their* responsibility to teach. Right?

In my childhood family's finances, we didn't have what we wanted because the government wouldn't increase our benefits. Food stamps only went so far, so our poverty was the politicians' fault, not ours. It was so much easier to sit back and point a finger at those whose responsibility it was to make our lives better rather than claim the responsibility for ourselves.

In my business relationships, I blamed not myself but my mentors for my lagging growth. I felt they weren't giving me enough guidance, and so my business struggles were their fault, not mine. It wasn't my responsibility to go out and find clients to serve and partners to mentor. Not when it was so much easier to have my mentors do my push-ups for me.

In my personal life, I felt joyless and unfulfilled because the people around me weren't changing. It was never my own fault that I was unhappy, because *I* was not responsible for my personal happiness—*they* were! So, because others around me weren't growing past their own negative patterns, destructive behaviors, and poor attitudes, my own happiness was somehow an impossibility. As I liked to say, it wasn't my fault.

Do you see the disconnect? Do you see the limitations of my own beliefs, my own clay?

The belief that "it isn't my fault" puts us in the passenger seat of our own lives. It strips us of responsibility and allows us to remain passive instead of taking action. Passive is easy—all we need to do is sit around and wait for things to fall into our laps. There is no need to take action and chase what we want or claim our responsibility.

But the downside is … despite our own delusions and wishful thinking, what we want rarely (if ever) falls into our laps.

For some reason, I was willing to put in thousands of hours and millions of reps to transform myself into the elite baseball player I was obsessed with becoming. I took on that responsibility and fully understood that if I failed, it was not anyone's fault but my own.

Yet in every other area of my life, my lack of success was *someone else's fault*. I was blind to my own responsibility and my role in my success, just as I was blind to my own clay. Worse, it seemed to be a kind of *selective* blindness. I was choosing—consciously or unconsciously—where I wanted to take action, and where I wanted to place blame.

How messed up is that mindset?

Eventually, when I was around thirty years old, I finally made the connection. I finally understood that there was a direct link between effort and success. I finally realized that there was *more than one type of push-up.*

They said, "Don't wish things were easier; wish you were better."

— THINK LIFE *is* DIFFERENT

I finally had what I now call the *second shift*.

I had done the work—the push-ups, the swings, the crunches, and more—to get where I wanted to be in athletics. And yet I wanted other people to do the push-ups *for* me in academics, finance, business, and even in my own personal happiness? That made zero sense.

I realized that in athletics and in all other aspects of life, *I had to do my own push-ups.*

ACTUALLY DOING THE PUSH-UPS

Realizing that I needed to do my own push-ups in life was a far cry from actually *doing* them.

You're going to laugh when I tell you this, but years ago, I was excited to get married. That's not the funny part. The funny part is … I was excited to get married because *I thought it would make my life easier*.

Keep laughing, I'll wait.

One of my problems is that I go into things with great expectations— and marriage was no different. I had this grand vision that my wife, Amanda, and I were going to be this highly successful power couple, wearing business suits and dominating the local, national, and even international scene. We were both going to make equally incredible amounts of money and split all of life's decisions and responsibilities right down the middle. Everything was going to be equal. Everything was going to be perfect.

But … that's not how it happened. That's not how it *ever* happens. As you read in Shift One, Amanda and I didn't want the same things out of life. We didn't even interpret success in the same way. For me, success was wrapped up in money and drive, whereas for her it meant comfort and stability. Neither of these interpretations was right or wrong. They were just *different*.

But I couldn't see that at the time. I was working hard. I wanted *more*. And I wanted Amanda to pick up the slack. I wanted her to help me make my perfect dream come true. And to my frustration, she wasn't doing it. All I could see was that she was abandoning me in my dream for us to be successful together.

It probably didn't help that, at the same time, I was battling with my spirituality and my belief in God. I was a good guy who did good things and made good decisions. But there was all of this *bullshit* going on in my life. I began to wonder: did God love me? Did God even *care* about me at all? Where was He at? Not on my side, obviously.

All of this culminated in a two-year depression during which the days were dark and the nights were darker. I stopped taking care of myself. I gained weight. I lost money. My relationship with Amanda was tense and uncomfortable, and we began to have conversations about divorce. I felt terrible all the time.

Then I got lucky. Out of the blue, a friend reached out to me and offered to help me get healthier physically. It's never flattering to have someone point out the depths to which you have sunk, but in this case, it was exactly what I needed. The revelation of my own failure helped me break through it.

They say that one good decision or habit leads to the next good decision or habit, and it's absolutely true. Once I started eating better, I started hydrating better, then sleeping better, and finally feeling better. Every step I took dragged me just a little bit more out of the dark spiral I had traveled down.

Now, it wasn't easy. I had to very intentionally take each step, and no one could take those steps for me. I was right back to having to do my own push-ups—this time, literally.

WE WANT TO BE BETTER

I love having a coaching business, and I love the coaching business model. Every day, I am fortunate enough to work with incredible people and hear the stories they don't usually tell anyone else. I get to peek behind the curtain into what things are really like for even the most successful individuals.

Now, no matter how successful or unsuccessful they may be, most people generally want to be *better*. The problem comes when we don't know *how* to be better—or *what* "better" even looks like.

This was absolutely true in my case as well. I didn't know how to become a better person, or what "better" really meant in concrete terms for me, so I would simply remain in what I perceived to be a comfortable place (a.k.a., my comfort zone) until it got to the point where I was either inspired enough or desperate enough to try and change my situation. However, inevitably a strain of helplessness would seep in, and I would return to my comfort zone, largely unchanged and unmoved.

When I first started coaching, I began to see similar trends in my clients. They would get going down a path of enlightenment and transformation … and within a day, a week, a month, three months … they would quit.

When they quit, I would ask them why, and the responses I received were extremely telling:

- *"My spouse doesn't have the same regimen as me."*
- *"My manager changed my schedule."*
- *"My in-laws were in town that weekend."*
- *"My friends were making fun of me."*
- *"I'm waiting for my tax refund."*
- *"I didn't get as much back from my tax refund as I needed."*
- *"My business partner quit."*
- *"My vacation to Europe is coming up."*
- *"My kids … [fill in the blank]."*

In each and every one of those excuses, I heard the echoing refrain: *"It's not my fault."*

They said, "STOP spending all your time working on your job and spend more time working on yourself. If you work at your job, you'll make a living. If you work on yourself, you'll make a fortune because of whom you'll become."

— THINK LIFE *is* DIFFERENT

"IT'S ALL MY FAULT."

Hear me out: what if it *is* your fault?

What if your success and the ability to reach your goals is all *your* responsibility and not someone else's?

What if your happiness is *not* predicated on someone else doing the work for you, with you, or through you?

What if you didn't have to wait for someone else to make your own life or your business better (whatever "better" means for you)?

What if your lack of success AND happiness is not *someone else's* fault?

What if it's *your* fault?

And what if you *accepted* that fault openly, and with no arguments, and changed your behavior because of it?

Don't worry—it took me a long time to internalize all of this too. But once I did, my success knew no limitations. Before that, though, I was doing a lot of the silly things that we tend to do when we feel like nothing is our fault.

I remember a time when I had a big leadership conference coming up—my very first one. I was excited about it, but I was also in a place where I was not taking personal responsibility for my own successes and failures. I was in the same place many of my clients had been, where I was blaming everyone around me for my frustrations. My mentors and confidants had abandoned me. No one was giving me the answers or the support I needed. Because of this, because of *these people*, and by no fault of my own, my business and life were not growing.

So, I acted out accordingly. I began to place blame … on everyone but myself. I began to passive-aggressively text my so-called friends, mentors, and confidants. I began to delete them off of Facebook. I showed them how upset I was by not getting back to them in a timely manner when they reached out. Surely, I thought, this would teach them a lesson.

As it turned out, many of my colleagues whom I had shunned turned up at the big leadership conference. So, I decided to *continue* teaching them a lesson there. I gave them the cold shoulder. When they approached me, I looked the other way. When I saw them out in public, I would duck and act like I didn't see them. It felt like the perfect opportunity to show them just how much they had hurt me.

Ironically, I was doing this *in the literal context of a leadership conference.* As I attended the conference sessions, classes, and talks, all led by leaders I admired, it began to dawn on me how ignorant I had been. It began to dawn on me that my behavior was not leaderlike. That I was not being a leader.

Leaders take responsibility.

Leaders do their own push-ups.

Leaders don't sit around, waiting for all of the people and circumstances around them to magically change.

Leaders don't base their happiness or success on whether other people can assist them in the exact way they want.

Leaders don't get what they want by waiting for Lady Luck to find her way to their door.

Leaders learn to see things differently.

Leaders *act.*

In fact, leaders act like I did *back in my childhood baseball days.* Back when I was taking my swings without a coach telling me to do so. Back when I was doing my sit-ups every day, regardless of whether the sun came out. Back when I was doing my push-ups regardless of whether I felt like it. Back when I was practicing my swings whether or not my friends came over to join me.

Back when, if I didn't practice, and if I didn't become the baseball player I wanted to become, *it was my fault.*

The hard truth I didn't want to own was that my lack of success in my business and life was *my fault*. The even harder truth was that I had to *own* that truth, accept it, and finally begin to move past it.

Whether you like it or not, this hard truth—and the harder truth—pertains to you too. Own it with me. Accept that everything you don't like about your life right now is *your fault*.

Even if it's not *actually* your fault.

That's the key. That's what it means to accept responsibility. Even if you can argue that you didn't get yourself into this mess, or that something bad happened to you beyond your control, or that it's *not actually your fault*—you can *say* it is. That is how you *begin to control the narrative* and change the story. It's not fun, but it is necessary if you want things to change for the better.

So, if your business is failing to grow, you begin to say: it's your fault. If you have crappy relationships, it's your fault. If you are fat, if you are broke, if you are sad … it's your fault. If you're stuck in a job you hate, it's your fault. If your mortgage defaults, it's your fault. If you're a pastor and your congregation is nowhere to be found, it's your fault. If there's traffic on the freeway and you're freaking out about it, it's your fault. If your kid is a jerk, it's your fault. If it bothers you that your wife doesn't make the bed, guess what? *It's your fault.*

That's the bad news. But it's the good news too. Because if you change the story to say that you got yourself into this mess, then *you can get yourself out of it*. You have that power. Because you have *given* yourself that power.

You initially gave away your superpower by sitting around waiting, hoping, and praying that others would do your push-ups for you—but you can get it back. It cannot come from anyone or anywhere else. It has to be awakened and activated *within* you, *by* you, and *for* you.

I know it sucks. But say it with me: "It's *my* fault. And that's a *good thing*."

E + R = O

People come to me every day with issues that aren't their fault:

- *They get unfairly laid off from work.*

- *An earthquake or terrible fire destroys their home or business.*

- *Their friends and peers are not supportive of them.*

- *Their spouse is cheating on them.*

- *Their brother-in-law stole a significant sum of money from them.*

- *Their kids have [insert a multitude of reasons here, from soccer practice to the constant need for supervision].*

- *There is just not enough time in the day to do everything.*

Life is not fair, and it never *has* been. I get it, trust me—I was born poor and Black. But just because something isn't your fault *doesn't mean you can't take responsibility for it.*

I like to tell my clients, "Take control of your 'R.'" This is a reference to one of my favorite formulas: **E + R = O**, or, more fully spelled out, **Event + Response = Outcome**. It's a simple equation, but it's extremely effective. Let's break it down.

In life, events (E) *happen*, whether we want them to or not. That earthquake destroys your home, or you get unfairly laid off from your job. These events are often completely out of our control (though that doesn't mean we can't do anything about them).

We will inevitably have some kind of response (R) to these events. Now, unlike the inciting event itself, we *do* have complete control over our response. In response to the earthquake, you could choose to rage against the heavens, sink into despair, and cancel the mission-critical business meeting you had scheduled for that Friday. Or you could choose to take a deep breath, file your insurance claim, ask a friend or family member if they'll be able to put you up for a few days, and show up for that meeting regardless.

Each response (R) leads to a different outcome (O). The first leads to a loss for your business, relationship, sanity, happiness, faith, mission, passion, or purpose. The second is potentially a win.

The outcome (O) is not determined by the event (E) alone. And it cannot happen without the response (R). *It is the R that makes the difference.* It's in the R that the miracles can happen. So, when you take control of your R, *you can take control of the outcome of any situation,* good or bad.

I have to tell you—a very capable man came to me the other day, complaining about how he's two months behind on his rent. But it's not his fault, of course—it's his *wife's* fault. She turns away business because she wants a higher price point, so they are not making their revenue goals.

In this example, where **E + R = O**:

- *E: The wife is turning away smaller clients.*

- *R: The man apparently does nothing, other than complaining to me and acting like the victim, convincing himself that she doesn't love him, doesn't care about their marriage, is selfish, and is trying to be the "head" of the household.*

- *O: The man is approaching a mild depression; he is frustrated, crying, two months behind on his rent, and asking to borrow money.*

This man's trouble with his business and his rent is *his* fault and no one else's. He could have chosen to respond (R) in a number of different ways that would have produced a better outcome (O). He could have hustled during those two months to find clients who could pay the higher price point. He could have had a conversation with his wife about client standards and their overall business plan. He could have injected money from another account (or, if they had no other accounts or a time machine, planned better in the first place … but I digress). He could have seen this situation as an opportunity from God to take the next steps in his growth, leadership, and ability to produce. He could have told himself that this is happening "for him" and not "to him." He could have chosen to see this as a blessing and not a curse. It's nothing more or nothing less than a perception opportunity.

The point is, this man did not take control of his R. He completely wasted that opportunity when he came crying to me instead of taking responsibility and taking action. He stayed where he was—where he was *comfortable*—and let success pass him by.

Now, I don't want to sound too harsh. I've been there. We've *all* failed to take control of our R at some point. In the not-too-distant past, people may have heard me say things like, "I'm broke, and it's all my wife's fault." Or, "I'm fat because Amanda won't go to the gym with me."

So, in terms of our **E + R = O** equation:

- *E: I'm fat.*
- *R: I get emotional, blame, point fingers, and complain that it's my wife's fault.*
- *O: I'm still fat, and I'm still mad, and we don't speak for a few weeks.*

It doesn't really work, does it? But if I take Amanda out of the equation and take responsibility myself, then you can see:

- *E: I'm fat.*
- *R: I take responsibility, look at it as an opportunity for growth, change my eating habits, and do my push-ups.*
- *O: I feel empowered, and I look and feel great! I build self-confidence.*

That little letter *R* makes a huge difference. But we have to *make* it make a difference.

We *love* finding the fault in someone else and pointing that finger of blame. It's so easy to move over from the driver's seat to sit in the passenger's seat. Plus, if it's someone else's fault, that means we don't have to think of solutions or be held accountable in any way. We just get to be upset and point a finger, and maybe enjoy a little bit of pity or righteous indignation while we're at it.

But … along the same lines, if it's someone else's fault, it's not *our* problem, so there is no reason for *us* to change or even act. If it's *someone else's* fault, then *we* don't have to swing that bat 1,095,000 times to get better. If it's someone else's fault, *we* are out of the picture entirely.

And we've lost the opportunity to make our second shift.

If we really and truly want to change our lives for the better, we need to learn to take control of our R. We need to claim our power. And as we'll explore in the upcoming sections, *even if something is not your fault, treat it like it is.* Accept responsibility. Take action. And move forward. Great outcomes *will* follow.

OTHER PEOPLE'S PUSH-UPS

I still remember the day, back when Amanda and I were dating, that Amanda dropped the bomb on me that she thought it would be a great idea for us to move in together.

Now, I did *not* think it was a great idea. It wasn't logical. It wasn't practical. And I had gotten used to having my own space and doing things the way I liked to do them.

Back when I was growing up, my mom had always invited people to stay at our home, from my oldest brother to my uncle Sunny. These guests would inevitably end up with me in my room … which was not a real room at all but rather a partitioned section of the dining room.

The year before Amanda suggested moving in together, a friend of mine who was an interior design specialist had helped me transform my one-room bachelor pad into the type of space I had always dreamed of. It was visually stunning. The walking distance from my bed to the bathroom was ideal. The curtains were at a perfect 90-degree angle. The best part, though, was my bed. I made it before I left for work every single day, and it was *flawless.* I cannot fully express the depth of love and appreciation I had for the look and feel of my own living space, so believe me when I say it was perfect.

Then Amanda moved in. And I quickly learned that not everyone shares the same ideals for a living space.

Amanda and I had a completely different philosophy of cleanliness and what a room should look like when you leave it. My idea of cleanliness was a room ready for showcasing on HGTV. Her idea was, "I want someone to walk in and see what it looks like after a tornado sweeps in from Kansas."

This move brought a tremendous amount of tension and chaos into our relationship. It was the first time I had ever lived with a woman I was dating, and it turns out I was not ready to handle it. I would get up in the morning for work, survey the messy room, and just *glare* at Amanda in frustration. She was messing up my flow, my jam! Believe it or not, some of our earliest and most intense arguments were over something as small as making the bed.

Every day for months, I would leave for work in a cloud of frustration. And every day, I came home, hoping against hope that Amanda had changed her habits of the last twenty-plus years and suddenly fit into my paradigm of proper neatness. (Spoiler: it never happened.)

This went on for *two years*.

Two years of frustration, tension, and constant arguments as I prayed that Amanda, now my fiancée, would receive some kind of message from above to change her messy ways. Or maybe an intervention would be a better idea …

Or—as it occurred to me one day out of the blue—maybe I could do my own damn push-ups.

The sudden realization stung—that I could only do *my own push-ups* and *no one else's*. That I only had control over one person in my life, and that was *me*. That I had the power and responsibility to change *myself* and *no one else*.

I had wanted Amanda to change to suit my standards, my wants, my *flow*. But her life isn't about me. Her life is about *her*. If Amanda was going to change, it would only be when *she* was ready and willing to do so.

You cannot do someone else's push-ups. You can't even tell someone else what their push-ups *are*—or *"should" be*. You can only do your own push-ups, encourage others to discover theirs, and learn to be satisfied with that.

FIND THE GOOD

So, what did it mean to do my own push-ups in response to Amanda's messy habits? How was I able to change my R to the E and learn to make peace with something I hated?

I had to learn to find the good in every E and focus on that.

For every event we consider "bad," there is something that is "good"—a yin and a yang, a push and a pull, an up and a down, a left and a right. For whatever reason, life has its dichotomies, and the "good" and "bad" are present in every situation (every E) to balance each other out. In every E, both good and bad must exist. In every E, there lies a potential test for you to discover your own weaknesses and the stronger stuff you're made of.

The ideas of "good" and "bad" in each E are also largely subjective, up to our interpretation, mindset, and perspective. And the one that looms larger generally does so because we focus on it.

In my situation with Amanda, I was forced to consider: was her not making the bed a morally "good" or "bad" thing? Not really. Was it even *that big of a deal*, in the grand scheme of life? Not really. In relation to every other problem in the world, Amanda's inability to make the bed was admittedly a very small problem. So … why was I letting it get me down?

As they say, "You can always tell the size of a man by the size of the problem that gets him down." I was acting like a small person with a small mindset. I was having a disproportionate and thoughtless R to the E at hand.

To paraphrase Jim Rohn, "Some people don't do well in life because they *major* in minor problems." That was me. I was majoring in minor problems. I was giving disproportionate attention to this very small problem and allowing it to control my mood, my thoughts, my behavior, my relationship, and, ultimately, my *life*.

I began to wonder: What if it's all just a test to see who I am? What if I were to shift my mindset and begin to treat all of these "problems" and situations as a test to see who I am?

Whether the E is large or small, the trick comes in realizing *you can overcome it* with thought and focus. The size of the E doesn't matter, despite how much larger some problems may *seem* when compared to others. Those smaller-seeming Es—say, level one to five out of ten— seem easier to deal with because, chances are, we've dealt with them before, and we know how to shape our R to serve our O when they come around. But if it's a level six to ten E, it might be new territory for you, something you haven't had to deal with before. Something like someone very close to you dying unexpectedly. That's a level six to ten E, but it's still an E, and therefore, you can learn to *always* see the good in it. The truth of the matter is, the unknown terrifies us, and that terror makes "problems" seem bigger and often more negative than they actually are.

Often, when we're lost in the terrifying unknown, our R can be thoughtless because we're focused on our fear instead of how we're responding to the issue at hand—or we're so occupied that we're simply not thinking clearly. Those thoughtless Rs can include wanting to blame, point fingers, make excuses, say "I can't," or simply procrastinate indefinitely. It also includes eating your feelings, yelling at your spouse, kicking at the dog, flipping the bird at someone who cut you off in traffic, indulging in self-pity, having a few too many drinks to dull the pain, and putting the rest of your money on black ... only to lose it.

Thoughtless Rs like these are harmful in the long run, even though they may often be satisfying in the moment. Ultimately, however, they will cause you to strain your relationship with your spouse, go broke, get fat, look bad, and more. Thoughtless Rs will keep you from the greater good—from growing, learning, and overcoming the stuff that will return time and time again in your life to hold you back. You will get a negative O from a negative R.

A thoughtful R, on the other hand, will serve your future health and happiness—and result in a positive O. Thoughtful Rs are often tough to think of and even more difficult to implement. They usually involve taking the high road; accepting the fault, blame, or responsibility for a situation; deferring gratification; and other things that aren't incredibly pleasant in the moment.

It was easy to settle on a thoughtless R when considering my E of Amanda's inability to make the bed, and for a long time, I did. Frustration, resentment, arguments, subtle and less-subtle hints ... all thoughtless Rs, all easily available when I reached for them. And of course, they all resulted in a negative O of tension, additional frustration, arguments, and more.

They said, "You will fully arrive once you get to a place where you see the good in every situation. Yes, even death."

— THINK LIFE *is* DIFFERENT

Earlier, we talked about how there is a balance to everything. In every situation, there is both "good" and "bad," completely subject to our mindset and interpretation. I began to notice that, when I focused on the "bad" stuff, I leaned toward thoughtless Rs that resulted in negative Os. But what would happen if I discovered and focused on the good in every situation, in every E?

Was there a silver lining to Amanda not making the bed? Could all of the things I considered to be "flaws" in Amanda—including her frustrating messiness—be reinterpreted as blessings in disguise? And could I still love her regardless? The answer is absolutely yes.

It was more difficult to be thoughtful than thoughtless, but in the end, I learned how to put in the thought, find the good in every situation, and choose the thoughtful R. It all had to do with the O—did I want it to be positive or negative? It was all within my control. I could coast on instant gratification and choose the thoughtless, or I could put in the work, choose the positive, thoughtful R, and enjoy a meaningful O.

It all came down to what was *best serving the outcome*—and what would best serve my future health and happiness.

So, ask yourself: what is the good in every E? What can you focus on that is positive? How can your thoughts better serve *your* future health and happiness? Can you get really good with saying, "Is this thought serving me?" Can you answer that question honestly, and if the honest answer is no, can you get to a place where you can always start to change that thought, so your answer can be yes? There you'll find your superpower. And it'll NEVER matter what the E is.

THE DOUBLE-EDGED SWORD OF HELP

Going into 2013, I wanted to expand my network and my coaching business. I'd had an awakening about how to better connect with people and guide them toward the solutions they were searching for, and I was eager to help as many people as possible.

I put in some work on my business plan and realized that the way to grow my business was not to solely focus on working with my own personal clients but to attract many more business partners—all I had to do what find out what people *truly wanted*. (Yeah … that was "all" I had to do. Easier said than done, especially in the context of our earlier discussion that most people don't have any idea what "better" looks like for their lives. But I digress.)

Human beings are more alike than we are different. We all have the same essential core desires, in the sense of Maslow's hierarchy of needs—beyond the basics of food, clothing, and shelter, we all want to feel safe, loved, and valued. Everyone is looking for *something* related to those needs, and I made that *something* my business.

In these modern times, that *something* often translates to gaining more money and more time and losing both stress and weight. I knew I could help people do that, and I had perfected the skillset I needed to do so. However, I needed to do it at scale, and at the time I had only been able to bring on six new coaching partners over a six-month period. My new mindset and my new vision for my business demanded more. So, I laser-focused on expanding my coaching team, and I was able to bring on *thirty-five new coaching partners in two months*.

It was incredible, and at first, I was overjoyed at my massive success. I was going to be able to scale my business beyond what I had dreamed. The only problem was … I didn't know what to *do* with all of my new partners. While they had the energetic personalities and leadership traits I had been searching for, they all needed to be officially *trained* as coaches and leaders. And there were so many of them that I didn't know where to start.

Essentially, I had sown the seeds and enjoyed a plentiful harvest of crops, but I didn't know what to do with the crop. In this metaphor, I realized I didn't even know how to cook.

Fortunately, I did have a mentor who was a master chef (metaphorically speaking), who often did some cooking for those who didn't know how. I went to her with a proposition that I felt would be mutually beneficial. I said, "I have all of these new people—do you mind if I acquire them and you coach them, turn them into leaders?"

But to my surprise, her response was *no*. Or, more specifically, it was, "I won't do it for you, but I will show you how to do it."

I was completely blown away. She had done something similar for other people, so why not me? I had thirty-five new people to train, and obviously, there was no way I could do it all myself. So, I went back and begged, "Will you do it for me? Please?"

But the answer was the same: "No. I won't do it for you. But I will show you how to do it."

As I returned to my office, still shell-shocked from the rejection, I began to wonder: How come no one would help me? Did they not want my business (or their business) to grow? Did my mentor see me as competition? Was she betraying me? As her mentee, wasn't I entitled to her help? Had I made the mistake of trusting yet another authority figure who would abandon me to fend for myself?

As time went on, these questions continued to gnaw at me, and I grew more and more upset. No one wanted to help me. My confirmation bias pointed out all the ways that people had failed to help me in the past. The people I thought were here to help me had carelessly cast me aside when I needed them most.

Finally, I said, "Forget it. I'm going to stop bringing on more coaches. And those thirty-five new coaches I just brought on? They can go ahead and die on the vine. They're not going to be trained, they're not going to be successful, and it's all because no one will help me."

I stayed in this negative headspace for about a week, enjoying the feeling of righteous indignation just as much as I hated it. Eventually, I realized I didn't want to feel like this anymore, so I said, "Forget it. I'm going to write you guys off and figure out how to do it myself."

It felt good to say that, to declare my independence. It was something I had done before, when I traded in my baseball dreams for track and field, or when my mother wouldn't give me an allowance, and I decided, "No problem, I'll earn the money myself." This time, I decided I was going to learn how to train the coaches myself.

Determined to succeed, I stayed up later, reading more books and watching more videos. I asked more questions and had more tough conversations. I delved deep into what motivated people and, over time, even began to understand (and process) my own mindset. I stayed at the gym longer, and I did my own damn push-ups.

And as I grew into the person I had needed to be all along, I finally began to realize that I had been asking my mentor to do my push-ups *for* me. And I had been *angry* when she wouldn't.

Wow. Talk about entitlement posturing. I had been taking that passive seat and waiting for help to fall into my lap. I had been expecting success without putting in the work. I had been looking to grow *without actually growing.*

Even now, I look back on that and can't believe what I had been asking my mentor to do. By asking her to do the work for me instead of enabling me to learn for myself, I was asking her to take away my ability to see and develop my own gifts. I was asking her to take away my ability to understand that *I had another superpower.*

That superpower was self-sufficiency. Self-sufficiency means taking *radical responsibility* for your life. It means doing your own push-ups and taking charge of your own success. It means taking care of your own house, folding your own laundry, and making the bed every day. It means pushing past passivity and comfort and owning up to your faults. It means taking control of your R. It means setting impossible goals for your life and business and working hard to meet them.

Here's the kicker: All of those other people my mentor did the work for? Today, they are in no better situation than they were six years ago. They didn't do the work themselves, so they didn't grow. They didn't change. They are stuck because they don't know how to move forward on their own. And now several of them are coming to *me* for help.

We must move away from the mentality of people doing everything for us. Now, that's not to say you can't ask for help when you need it or that you can't hire assistants or employees. But when you need to make a major shift in your life or your business, that is work that you need to do yourself. No one can do that work for you.

And if you're sitting around, wishing, hoping, and praying that someone will come along and do the work for you, you're going to stay seated. So, unless you want to stay where you are, in that comfortable seat that takes you nowhere, take radical responsibility for your life. Build the muscle. Put in the hard work. And learn to fly.

THE SHIFT TO DOING YOUR OWN PUSH-UPS

Taking radical responsibility does not negate the magnitude of your obstacles or hardships. It empowers you to choose the right decisions and create a formidable life in the midst of them.

If I could leave you with just one takeaway from this entire book, it comes here (yes, as early as the second shift): *Do your own push-ups.* They're not comfortable, and they're not fun, but they are the catalyst for the change you are looking for.

That change you're seeking in your life or business is yours and yours alone to create. This whole thing is on *you*, and it's your responsibility to put in the work, claim your R, and learn to say, "It's my fault."

Even when it's not your fault, treat it like it is. Seizing fault —or responsibility or blame or whatever you want to call it—will reward you with the opportunity to find that next gift and brilliant thing you have inside … the gold beneath the clay. Doing your own push-ups is a mindset and a mentality that you must become victorious over. It is about becoming the surgical master of your mind.

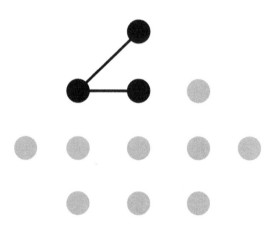

Shift Three

Find Your Land of Plenty

"It doesn't matter how smart you are unless
you stop and think."

– THOMAS SOWELL

Look, I get it. You can't afford it. It's too expensive. There's not enough money out there. You don't earn enough. The man is trying to keep you down. It's not possible to attain financial wellness (if it even exists). It's an absolute *must* to have two incomes per household in order to make it these days. Money doesn't grow on trees. What do they think you are made of, money? Money is the root of all evil … or wait, is *love* of money the root of all evil? I guess it doesn't matter—it's evil.

I already know, and I agree with you—everything is just too expensive. You can't find the right job. Absolutely no one is hiring. You're right; living in abundance means you probably don't care about humanity, morality, or civility. I'm right there with you. You're probably right.

Or are you?

All of the above thoughts, sayings, and beliefs have run through my head at one point or another. Some of my favorite phrases used to be, "I can't afford it," and "It's too expensive." But I've changed, and I'm confident that you can too.

We're all raised in a society that has a lot of issues with this thing called *money*. For most of us, I have found we are essentially trained from a very young age to have a weird, dysfunctional relationship with this thing that isn't even, in a sense, tangibly *real*. Money is just as much real as it is a figment of our imaginations, an invisible bartering tool that carries different emotional value based on how much or how little of it we possess.

It was also inextricable from my understanding about morality, charity, and service. In a way, I felt good about money, and yet I felt bad about it. I wanted it, yet I didn't want it. I desired it but felt like I would go to hell if I had too much of it. I lived in the wealthiest nation on the planet, yet every day, I saw living examples of extreme poverty. I was struggling financially myself, and often found myself repeating those phrases: "I can't afford it," and "It's too expensive," while some of my friends and family members seemed easily able to live the lives of their dreams.

In my published work *The Richest Man in Direct Sales*, I outline what Amanda and I did to begin building wealth—the strategies we used,

They said, "Be a happy taxpayer."

— THINK LIFE *is* DIFFERENT

the budgets we set, the vision we had, the disciplined actions we took, and the delayed gratification that we became married to. This book will not rehash that information; instead, we'll be taking a look at the mindset and psychology behind what it means to rethink our dysfunctional relationships with money and live in true abundance.

THE ROOT OF THE MINDSET

The stories we tell ourselves about money take root early on in life. These stories are generally planted by our parents and caretakers and further cultivated by our environment. They grow, often insidiously unseen, below the surface of our awareness, branching out and affecting us in surprising ways throughout our lives.

My money story originated with my family's pastor, though it was later reinforced by others, including my friends and relatives. This relationship came from a passage I heard growing up in church over and over again: "The love of money is the root of all evil."

Now, our pastor may have said it that way, and the sentiment of the congregation probably postured it that way, but … somehow, I missed it. Somehow, what I heard as a child was an equation of money with evil. The Bible itself even says in Mark 10:25 that, "It is easier for a camel to go through the eye of a needle than for a rich person to enter the kingdom of God." Luke 6:20 further reinforces this mindset, telling us that, "Blessed are you who are poor, for yours is the kingdom of God."

In my mind, there was a clear "us vs. them" divide between the rich and the poor—the "haves" and the "have nots." The "haves" had stuff—money, cars, land, the ability to purchase first-class airline tickets, and all of the other privilege that came with those things—and the "have nots" did not. Yet the "have nots" would be compensated for their earthly suffering in heaven, where they would inherit the kingdom of God, while the "haves" (as my child's mind interpreted it) roasted in hell.

My family and I were "have nots," being poor and Black like our fellow churchgoers. We were good, wholesome folks who gave back to the poor, did community-service projects, checked on Sister Andersen after Sunday service, and generally led virtuous lives. We took solace in the fact that, while we lived in poverty and suffering on Earth, we would one day enjoy vast, eternal wealth in heaven.

The "haves," on the other hand, were corrupt. They were selfish, greedy, and cared only about themselves. They lied, extorted, and did not live virtuous lives, which meant that they were probably going to hell.

With "have" and "have not" being my two options to choose from (either in my head or in reality), there grew a dissonance. Morally and virtuously, how could I strive for great economic wealth? I wanted to be a "good" person. I wanted to inherit the kingdom of God. And yet, I faced a very real and insatiable hunger for what my congregation deemed "worldly treasure"—wealth, success, and all of its trappings.

Thus, two parts of me were born, and for years, they waged an intense battle of good and bad, right and wrong, heaven and hell, virtue and iniquity.

Mind if we dive a little deeper down the rabbit hole? This dichotomy wasn't just rooted in my church life—it made itself known at home too.

I remember that the matriarchs of my family used to say things like, "What do you think I'm made of, money?" and "Money doesn't just grow on trees, you know!" Over the years, I internalized these concepts, and they continued to shape my reality. I grew even more fond of two phrases that I heard and used often. They knew me well, and I knew them. We embraced one another, and their truth was my truth:

Phrase #1: "That's way too expensive!"

Phrase #2: "I (we) just can't afford that!"

The stage had been set.

THE KINGDOM OF GRAHAM

Remember that friend back in your childhood who would do anything for you? They were your loyal, trustworthy confidant, the person who knew *everything* about you and yet still wanted to be your friend.

You felt comfortable, secure, and uplifted around them, and the two of you generally shared the same ideas and opinions about things. In almost every single area, they represented who you were and mirrored your ideals and philosophies. But … there was still one small thing they did that would bug the crap out of you.

Maybe it was the way they chewed their gum, maybe it was the way they moved their mouth after they got braces, maybe they had a verbal tic you couldn't stand, or maybe it was their body posture as they stood idle. Maybe they had a weird sneeze that sounded like a baby finch, and worse, they never sneezed just once or twice in a row like a normal person but rather indulged in a third, fourth, and fifth sneeze that inconvenienced your life. Remember that?

As a young boy, I had all the qualities of a good friend. Loyalty, check. Sincerity, check. Trustworthiness, check. Compassion, check. Empathy, check. And yet, I had a weird idiosyncrasy, too, that one small thing that often got the better of me. I was a liar.

You think Pinocchio's nose was long? Mine could probably have anchored a few buildings together. I lied as frequently and fluidly as a used-car salesman. It was a constant for me, and I became so good at telling made-up stories that I actually began to believe them.

Oddly enough, I didn't lie about *everything*. I mean, a guy has to have some sort of standards, right? I had a niche and owned one particular space in the marketplace of lies. I knew I was an "us"—a "have not"—and, if it meant being categorized as an "us" or a "them," I *always* lied about my "us"-ness.

Allow me to explain.

My buddy Graham was one of my very best friends in fifth and sixth grade. He and his family were part of the "them" (the "haves") tribe, but, to be fair, in my mind, anyone who could drive through a McDonald's and consistently order the too-expensive Happy Meals was a "them" to me.

Graham was unique in that he was not only affluent but highly generous, extremely modest, and supremely humble. Which was strange, because I knew that the "thems" of the world were supposed to be greedy savages destined for a fiery death. But I digress.

Graham was one of those all-American boys who just seemed to have everything going for him. The hair, the style, the personality, the baby-blue eyes, two parents in the home, and enough new shoes to get a person through five winters. He always had the absolute coolest MTV pop-culture T-shirts, and, when Valentine's Day or Easter rolled around, I knew he would bring in all the goodies. Not just the cards but the fancy candy as well—the same for each of the thirty students in the class, yet individually styled to make each child feel like they stood out. Graham was a master of abundance, and I loved and envied it at the same time.

Being friends with Graham at school was a treat in and of itself. However, it did not even come close to the infinite awesomeness that being at his house brought. Forget the two dogs that were always perfectly groomed, the manicured grass, the sparkling cleanliness of the house, or the *two extra bedrooms* that lay dormant and unused. Let's just focus on the important stuff: the video game systems.

Back then, there was an ongoing battle of two or maybe three gaming systems. Atari was fading out and being replaced by Nintendo and Sega. Now, at that time, for most of us, these game systems were like Nike and Reebok—it would be ludicrous to have both, so you had to choose just one. And even then, having even just one gaming system at home made you royalty.

But Graham was on a *completely* different level. If the level he was on represented one of the four Buddhist stages of enlightenment, Graham was on stage four, *Arahant*. See, he was the kind of kid who didn't just go to Thrifty's for one scoop of ice cream. No, no. He went and got the whole pint. Similarly, he had a Nintendo. *But he had a Sega Genesis too.* That in itself was unthinkable.

Now, this is where it gets good. Graham had something else that all of the other kids could only talk about. There was a new handheld gaming system called the Game Boy that everyone wanted and only the Ferris Buellers of the world could attain. Ferris Bueller, and, apparently, Graham.

In my eyes, this elevated him to legendary status. For a fifth grader with my socioeconomic reality and my "we can't afford it" worldview, Graham was the closest thing to a demigod I could possibly imagine. Graham, in all his enigmatic demigod ways, forced me to sin and become a serial liar.

Okay, clearly, I'm being facetious. But at that time in my life, I felt trapped and helpless. My parents couldn't provide Nintendo and Sega systems (let alone a Game Boy) for me like Graham's parents could, so how was I supposed to fit in with him? If A equals B, and B equals C, then A equals C. Graham and I were fundamentally unequal.

But I found a way to make us equal—I just had to lie. Picture Graham and I playing video games at his house …

Graham: "You're getting so good at this game!"

Jamil's lie: "I know! I've been practicing at home! Remember, I told you I got this same game a month ago?"

Jamil's truth: I did not own the gaming system, let alone the game.

Graham: "How long have your mom and dad been married?"

Jamil's lie: "About the same amount of time as your parents!"

Jamil's truth: My parents were never married and had all of their children out of wedlock.

Graham: "Is your dad going to come to our game this weekend?"

Jamil's lie: "I think so! I'll have to ask him again to make sure."

Jamil's truth: My dad was in prison and had been there for years. There was no way he was coming to our game.

Graham: "What does your mom do for work?"

Jamil's lie: "She's one of the top real estate agents in the Pasadena area."

Jamil's truth: My mother did not work, and we were on welfare.

Graham: "When do you think you are getting a Game Boy?"

Jamil's lie: "My mom said I could have it after she closes her next deal."

Jamil's truth: My mother and I had never discussed it.

Graham: "What are you doing for summer vacation?"

Jamil's lie: "We'll probably head up to our cabin and spend the majority of our time there."

Jamil's truth: There was no cabin.

Lies, lies, lies, all lies. It was risky and embarrassing, yet necessary (I thought) for me to blend into that aspirational environment. My family simply could not afford to have the things he had or to do the things his family did. This attitude, this philosophy, and this worldview all shaped the fabric of my mindset. I felt diminished, ashamed, and somehow *less* when I compared my life to his, and inventing my own largesse through lies helped to keep those feelings at bay.

The feelings were further complicated by the fact that Graham did not match up to the definition of "them"—a.k.a., the "haves"—that I had learned about in church. I knew the "haves" were supposed to be arrogant, greedy, and corrupt, but ... Graham was generous, kind, and modest. He was a true friend and always shared what he had with me. It made no sense.

Graham was everything he wasn't supposed to be, and, through our friendship, I gained a sort of economic counterbalance, a money story from a different point of view. I began to question the values of the money story that had been planted at my core. I had learned that wealth and virtue were incompatible, and yet, Graham somehow displayed both. What was it about his wealth that would keep him from passing through the metaphorical eye of the needle? What made him undeserving of inheriting the kingdom of heaven? Was his wealth inherently evil? And was my family inherently virtuous in our poverty ... or were we simply good people who could not afford the same things Graham had? What was true?

All I knew for certain was that my family simply did not have enough—we could not afford the things my best friend had.

But was *that* even the truth?

ALL YOU KNOW IS ALL YOU KNOW,
UNTIL YOU KNOW DIFFERENT

The saddest part about these lies is that they followed me into adulthood. The same propensity to "fit in" and become a "them" dogged my steps into my twenties and early thirties. Those deeply embedded roots, beliefs, and philosophies about money clung to me desperately.

Even though I had grown into this handsome, virile, strong, and independently thinking man, I still held onto fifth-grade habits and belief systems. I had always done "just okay" when it came to my careers and building up healthy finances. And to be fair, it was a *relative* "just okay." On the outside, people could see that I had a solid job with a great compensation package and above-average benefits. But ... that wasn't what I wanted. At the age of thirty-one, I still wanted my Graham experience.

Up until that age, I followed the rules: I graduated with honors from college and managed to get a job with Johnson & Johnson in the highly competitive market of pharmaceutical sales. I had a company car and an expense account, and, when people learned that I got to educate and influence doctors daily regarding the prescriptions they wrote for their patients, they seemed genuinely impressed.

However, I still wasn't where I wanted to be. The numbers on the checks mailed to my apartment looked really nice, but after I deposited the money into my bank account, the numbers somehow still weren't big enough. It was strange. Wasn't I playing the game right and doing things the "right" way? Wasn't I following all the rules? Then why was there so little margin at the end of each month? Where was my money going? Why did my forward progress seem so minimal?

My close friends were all starting to purchase houses and cars and other such items for their families, but *I* seemed to be stuck in my fifth-grade reality. Instead of envying Graham's Game Boy, I envied Tim's new house. Tim could somehow afford it, but me ... despite all I had earned and accumulated, I felt like I was still lying to myself and to others about how well I was doing. All I knew was all I knew.

They said, "Be a lender, not a spender."

— THINK LIFE *is* DIFFERENT

PRIORITIES AND WHAT WE CAN AFFORD

When I started my health coaching business, I had a realization that was as oddly comforting as it was unsettling. Sixty, seventy, eighty percent of the potential clients I spoke with would repeat the same refrain, day after day, week after week, month after month, all to the same tune: "I can't afford it."

The responses would vary, of course, but they were essentially all the same:

- *"That sounds great, but we're just a little behind and can't afford it right now."*

- *"Jamil, that sounds superb, and honestly I think it'll help me change my life, but we just can't afford it."*

- *"Yeah, I know I should do this, but the holidays are coming up, and I just don't know if I can afford it."*

A battle of uncanny dissonance settled in. On the one hand, I felt good, or at least justified—I wasn't alone! I wasn't the only person who felt like I couldn't afford what I wanted and needed! It was like these potential clients and I were long-lost brothers who randomly found one another after years of searching. But on the other hand, I was thinking, "Why the hell can't we afford the things that are so necessary and so affordable?" What in the doggone heck was truly happening here?

Facebook (which may or may not exist at the time you're reading this) finally helped me to have a real breakthrough. See, I was starting to move to a space of extreme pessimism—about my new business venture, about the individuals I spoke with, about my future success, and about the state of the country. If those of us who were playing by the rules couldn't make it, what about everyone else? Was there just no hope for any of us?

Fortunately, at that time, I started paying more attention to what people—and especially those prospective clients—were doing on Facebook. George "couldn't afford" health coaching services, but the pictures on his Facebook profile told me he had just taken his family of four to Disneyland in Anaheim. Sally "couldn't afford" it either but posted on Facebook about the cross-country trip she was taking with her husband to follow a cover band of the Beatles through eight different states and cities.

Bobby, an old college football buddy of mine, had met with me in a coaching capacity, saying he needed to get his life and his health in order. Later that day, he posted plans to take his family on a Caribbean cruise … just before he called me to say he "couldn't afford" my coaching services.

I meet with so many people who confess to me like I'm Father Frazier from St. Lucy's Catholic Church about why it's imperative that they contend for their health, but lament that they "can't afford" it right now. Then, sometimes literally the very next day, they post pictures of themselves buying rounds of drinks while out with friends.

Observing this behavior over and over again got me thinking about my own situation. Was it that I couldn't afford Graham's now-figurative Game Boy? Was it that I couldn't afford the house Tim just bought for his beautiful family? Were those "couldn'ts" and "can'ts" true? Or was it that my priorities were somehow … off? In what ways, I began asking myself, was I acting like George, Sally, and Bobby in my own life?

The truth was, most of the people whom I sat down with couldn't afford to NOT work with me. Their physical health—and their very lives—*depended* on it. And yet, for some reason, allocating money for short-term fun was more important than allocating money for long-term health. In a way, for these prospective clients, money held *more value than life.*

George had Disneyland, Sally had cover bands, Bobby had Caribbean cruises … so what did Jamil have? Slowly, I started taking inventory of the things in my life that were causing me to say, "I can't afford it" or getting in the way of me saying, "I *can* afford it" to anything as often as I wanted. What was I prioritizing in the moment? How could I better prioritize the things I wanted long-term? How could I make the right kinds of choices and sacrifices? What was the money story I was telling myself, and what was it rooted in? I was beginning to feel the small changes in my own priorities as I grew closer to the mindset shift I was about to make.

They told me, "Delay gratification. It will be hard. But for what you want, it will be necessary."

— THINK LIFE *is* DIFFERENT

DELAYED GRATIFICATION

When Amanda and I started our health coaching business and began attending continuing education seminars, one thing I kept hearing over and over was, "Get lean in your finances." We embraced this concept wholeheartedly and became obsessed with clearing out our debt, building up our savings and investments, and giving away at least 10 percent of our earnings monthly. We knew that living into a new money story would bring radical change to our lives.

Making the decision to live frugally was actually relatively easy. What *wasn't* easy was watching so many of my thirty-something friends move into the houses I desired, drive the cars I craved, and go on vacations I envied. It was hard to sit in their homes, looking at all of their nice things, knowing that, in a traditional sense, I could *technically* afford these things. But fighting the urge to run out and buy it took massive discipline.

When Amanda and I ended up purchasing our first property to live in, we bought it knowing that it was going to be an investment property down the road. It didn't have all the bells and whistles, but it made sense for us financially. It was far from our dream home, but that didn't matter at that moment—our goal was to live in the house for a couple of years *max* and then rent out the house while we moved into our next home.

Several years went by, and despite our frugal lifestyle and focus on saving and investing, we had not yet met our financial goals. We realized that we would need to stay in our current home for the foreseeable future. Even though I knew it wouldn't be forever, it was still intensely disappointing. I felt a deep sense of dissatisfaction and found myself obsessed with a future in which we could move into our dream home.

Frustration festered and became pessimism as the finish line (a.k.a. success … whatever *that* is) appeared to be moving farther and farther away, all while our friends continued to very visibly live the good life.

And the good life was *good*. Amanda and I would visit our friends in their beautiful homes, pretending for a while that we, too, had it all. The problem was that afterward, I couldn't stand walking back into my own bland little house. I dragged my feet over the threshold with incredible resistance, like nails running down a chalkboard. I hated it. I felt insignificant, humiliated, and even like a hypocrite. Here I was, a top leader in my business, supposedly doing well ... but I could not afford a home that matched my station.

Now of course, that was my own mental chatter, and everyone we knew probably thought our home was just fine. But remember: we make our own truths through our beliefs.

One evening, after spending a good amount of time with some friends in their dream home, I decided, "Enough is enough!" I couldn't take it anymore. I made the decision right then and there to rent out my house and move my family to a better home in a better city. The next day, I put our house on the market, started screening tenants, and drove for hours to scout out new homes in the new city.

Needless to say, this majorly inconvenienced my wife and kids, who had not been anticipating a very sudden move. The extra strain on my time left me making promises I couldn't keep, and my family was paying the price. But I told myself it was temporary, and remorselessly, I pushed forward.

I ended up finding a wonderful tenant who was the perfect fit to rent our house. In fact, she was even willing to pay *over* my asking price because she wanted to move in so badly. I ended up making promises to that poor woman that I could not keep. Not only that, but I found the *perfect* house for us to rent in the new city, which led me to make more promises that I knew I could not keep.

It didn't matter to me, though. I was ready, had made the decision to move, and was just relieved that I wouldn't feel judged anymore—least of all by myself. I wanted those nice things that I had denied myself for so long and felt I deserved. I had an itch that needed to be scratched *now!* I even convinced myself that the $700 more per month I'd be spending in this new location was justified—and wrote out a twelve-point list about *why* it was justified.

Everything was lining up: the nice house, the nice neighborhood, the nice things, the visible validation of my success that I had craved for so long. Everything I deserved was coming my way. There was just one small problem: I couldn't afford it.

A week or so later, my team, my mentors, and my wife were all out at a Christmas party in southern California. I was sitting alone on the couch when it hit me like a ton of bricks:

"Jamil, what are you doing?! The only reason you want to move is out of ego, pride, and appearances! Those are the *signals* of success, but they are not *true success*! What happened to your long-term goals? What happened to your vision of the future? What happened to building that foundation of true wealth? What are you living for? Do you want to be like so many others out there, looking good but going nowhere? Come on … you know this is not the right time for you. What you need to do now is stay focused, stay disciplined, and stick to your original game plan."

I call these self-talks "Conversations with Myself," and over the years they have been some of the most powerful conversations I've ever had. It's almost like God himself starts whispering to me, directing me, and mentoring me. Deep down, I knew it was not the right time for the actions I had taken—even *before* the conversation.

The problem was I couldn't control my ego. I couldn't wait. I had to have it now. I was still fighting the process in which things needed to happen. And with this realization came the second realization that *I needed to cancel this move*. It was refreshing to admit this, in a way, and it was so liberating to own the truth that I felt like a huge weight had been lifted off my chest.

But now it was time for some tough conversations. Remember the woman I'd promised I'd rent my house to? Well, she needed to be out of her own house in ten days and expected to be able to move into mine at that time. Her kids went to the same school my son went to, which meant that I'd have to face her even after the tough conversation about us staying put. I would also need to face the owners of the beautiful house I had intended to move into and tell them I was no longer able to make the commitment.

I was sick to my stomach, as I knew these conversations were impacting *real* people, and would have *real* implications on their stories moving forward. But … I had to do it. I had to delay my gratification. I had made the initial decision to move for the wrong reasons, because of my ego, pride, and hubris. I had decided my family needed to move, not because we *had* to, or because it was a smart financial investment, but because I thought moving would make me feel whole, complete, important, happier, loved … in short, *enough.*

But now I knew I needed to find those things independently of a fancy new house. To get those feelings, I would have to do a lot of serious work on and for myself. It would have to be an inside job. So … I did it. I canceled the move. I broke the promises. I refocused on my game plan. I learned a lot of *really* unpleasant lessons.

Three years later, we're still in our plain little house—but now we're ready to move into our dream home. And the satisfaction is there because this time, we did it in the *right way.* It's all about delayed gratification.

YOUR CIRCLE DETERMINES
HOW MUCH MONEY YOU MAKE

Recently, I had a conversation with my cousin, who is a mythical figure in my family. He was the first of us to graduate from college, after which he landed a job with a huge Fortune 500 company and worked his way up to a top management position. He's been relocated several times to wonderful cities to help spearhead new companies, and he and his wife were able to build their current home from the ground up, featuring five bedrooms, four-and-a-half bathrooms, and a grand total of 4,700 square feet. He travels frequently and basically lives a life that most people would go crazy for.

When my cousin called me and mentioned that he was considering doing what I do, I was curious, to say the least. He had always surrounded himself with professionals who were amazingly successful—top attorneys, dentists, presidents of companies, and the like. So, when he spoke with me over the phone that day, I did what I do best, and I listened.

I listened to how frustrated he was, not just with his work, but with his lack of mobility, time, freedom, and options. He felt as though he had reached the ceiling at his current company in his managerial position and was chafing under limitations. He shared with me how much he earned annually and how long and hard he had worked to get there.

Interestingly, my cousin told me that he felt *trapped by money*. While he *wanted* to pursue his passions and dreams, it did not seem like it would be worth disrupting his large and steady stream of income to do so. He believed it would not be financially responsible for him to do what he truly wanted. He was torn between feeling comfortable in his job and feeling stuck and frustrated, but he was too timid to overcome the fear and risk leaving his job. He was a classic example of someone who was living in a cage of his own creation—a scarcity mindset.

Something else happened during this conversation that was really eye-opening to me. I didn't anticipate telling my cousin how much Amanda and I were earning, but the conversation sort of took itself there anyway. I mentioned to him that we were earning on a *monthly* basis what he and most of his inner circle of friends were making *annually*.

"Jamil," he cried, astounded, "that's just *crazy!*"

And in a way, he was right. It *was* crazy. I couldn't believe it myself … except I *could*. Because *I had made it happen*. My cousin asked, "What do you attribute your success to?"

After a moment of reflection, I responded, "My environment."

In my cousin's inner circle, earning a certain amount of income was expected and deemed excellent, and that was what everyone in that circle earned. In my inner circle, the expected number was much, *much* higher. In my inner circle, I constantly looked up to giants and held myself accountable to their standards.

To my inner circle, the amount of money we were making wasn't "crazy." It was what we wanted, and we made it happen, doing the same work but scaling up the value. "Crazy" is subjective, and the line between millionaire and billionaire is tenuous when faced with an intentional mindset and a formidable inner circle.

Jim Rohn once famously said, "You are the average of the five people you spend the most time with," and he is absolutely correct. So, ask yourself: Whom do you want to be? How much money do you want to make? Surround yourself with people who are living the life you aspire to. The people you surround yourself with matter more than you know.

COACH WILL

A few months back, I had the opportunity to attend a training conference put on by some close friends. I was invited as a VIP guest and was allowed to sit at the very front of the room. All throughout the weekend, different people sat next to me, all extremely kind and cordial. One night, the president of a food delivery company sat next to me, and the next night, it was the president of the New York Stock Exchange. Another night, it was a very plain-looking woman who turned out to be a consultant for major brands like Mars, Nike, and Apple. It was like playing musical chairs with highly talented and successful people.

On one particular night, I found myself sitting next to a quiet gentleman and a very lovely woman who did enough talking for the entire table. The majority of her monologue was dedicated to the praise of someone named "Coach Will." It was Coach-Will-this and Coach-Will-that, all positive, of course, and while it struck me as slightly odd, I played along. Later, when the speaker from the stage partnered up the conference attendees for an abundance mindset exercise, wouldn't you know, I got partnered with Coach Will.

The exercise we did was designed to stretch our thinking and expectations and operate from an abundance mindset. Among other things in this exercise, we were instructed to write down our annual income and turn it into our *monthly* income. Then we were told to turn that monthly income into our *biweekly* income, our *weekly* income, and finally, our *daily* income.

I wrote down my numbers and dutifully shared them with Coach Will. He did the same, and I was surprised and impressed to see that Coach Will's starting number for his annual income was $8.8 million.

Just like my cousin had asked me, I asked Coach Will, "What do you attribute that number to?"

He responded, "You know, all of my friends and the people I spend most of my time with earn this and *more*. It matters who you surround yourself with. It matters a *lot*."

Later that night, after the conference had wrapped up, I googled "Coach Will" and saw that sure enough, his inner circle was filled with insanely successful people. My cousin's friends expected to make a certain amount, and so they did. My friends and my inner circle members expect to earn a certain amount, and we do. Coach Will and his circle expect to make a certain amount, and so they do. It's that simple. Your inner circle will largely determine how much you make.

HOW CAN I AFFORD IT?

The shift came at 3rd Street and Temple Avenue in Long Beach, California. The temperature that day was in the low seventies with a fresh breeze only the ocean could give. I had dropped off my son Ezra and spent some much-needed time at a yoga sculpt class. Everything about that day was normal … until it *wasn't*.

I returned to my condo, and, after an hour-long conference call, I turned on a personal development audio by one of my favorite speakers, Jim Rohn. I had heard this piece at *least* twenty times before and in all honesty was just turning it on for some white noise—but this time, the message *clicked* like it never had before, and I heard something entirely *new*.

Jim said that he used to say, "Things cost too much." Then his teacher straightened him out by saying, "The problem isn't that things cost too much. The problem is that you can't afford it." In shock, Jim (and I along with him) finally realized—the problem wasn't "it;" the problem was *me*.

That very same day, coincidentally, I listened to another speaker who said that if there is something out there you truly desire, you need to stop saying, "I can't afford it" and begin asking, "How can I afford it?"

On that day, in that 700-square-foot condo, with the cool ocean breeze blowing in … I shifted. I finally realized that the problem was *me*. I realized that I didn't need to go out and try to change everything *outside* of me; as we talked about in an earlier shift, I only needed to focus on changing myself. The only difference between "this costs too much" and "I can afford this" was *me*.

Financially, everything was possible. I could afford all things, if not now, then *at some point*. I didn't need to change anything outside of myself—not the prices of goods and services, not the meaning and value of money, all of which were outside of my control, anyway—I just needed to adjust my mindset from limitation and scarcity to abundance. I needed to evolve.

Once I realized I needed to evolve my mindset about money, wealth, and value, I quickly realized that I needed to change my expectations, relationships, philosophies, work ethic, ideas about purpose, and more— *it all needed to change*. I wanted the incredible feelings of possibility and abundance to permeate every single aspect of my life.

My main focus would no longer be on work and production—limited and limiting measurements—but on building the skills I needed to *evolve* my work. On reading the books I needed to read to expand my knowledge and expand my mind. I would focus on sitting through the tough conversations in full control of my R.

I would focus on listening to people intentionally and refrain from jumping in with an unasked-for response. I would watch Oprah interviews and learn how to build her style of immaculate rapport. I would listen to audio recordings of Dr. Martin Luther King, Jr. and study his dialect, his rhetoric, and his flow. I would maybe even muster up enough courage to contact or connect with the people who had inspired me over the years, people like Thomas Sowell and more.

I thought maybe the real rubric for success was how many no's could I take before I became disappointed and gave up? How much radical responsibility could I take? How much was I going to limit myself? What if there *was* no limit?

They said, "Profits are better than wages. Stop working for money and spend your time building assets. Leave everything and everyone you touch better than you found them."

— THINK LIFE *is* DIFFERENT

Our superpowers lie in wait deep within us—the gold latent beneath the clay—dormant until we reveal and activate them, often in moments of extreme desire or stress. After I recognized the abundance mindset within myself and made the shift to embrace and evolve into it, I realized that this superpower had always been there, deep within me, buried beneath layers of clay.

Before my wife and I were engaged to be married, we had never managed to save a large sum of money. It just wasn't top of mind at the time. But the moment we became engaged, it activated a sudden and intense desire to save up the money for the lavish and extravagant wedding we both wanted.

We dedicated ourselves completely to our financial goal, and even though neither of us was earning much at the time, we managed to put away *twenty thousand dollars in less than a year* in savings for our dream wedding. That's the power of the mind. That's the power of the abundance mindset—the subtle shift from "I can't afford it" to "How can I afford it?"

Ironically, after our wedding, try as we might, we were never able to save that much money again … until Amanda and I both intentionally shifted our mindsets and became aware of this superpower. Our attitudes and beliefs provided the discipline to perform the activities of success.

EZRA'S LEMONADE STAND

Throughout the years, I have worked with thousands of people who would claim, "I can't afford it," and "It's too expensive," about virtually everything. However, nothing had changed around them. Taxes were just about the same, the government was just about the same, poverty, education, unemployment, weather, opportunities, people who believed in them, people who didn't believe in them, interest rates, the number of people who had -isms (racism, sexism, ageism) … all the same.

Virtually everything was the same, and yet two, three, four, five years later, they could suddenly afford those things. How? Everything else was the same, but the key is that *they were not the same.* They had changed. They had taken the time to grow, to get better, become more, serve more people, and bring more value to the marketplace. And while it's fascinating to watch this change occur in adults, it's even more spectacular to witness it in kids.

My son Ezra is probably one of the best negotiators I know. As his seventh birthday drew closer, he told us that he wanted to host an extravagant birthday party at a Las Vegas-style venue for kids. Knowing his tendency to be tricky and slick, Amanda and I were quick to lay the ground rules. We would throw Ezra a traditional birthday party—the same as his other siblings—and if he wanted something larger, he could pay for that himself.

Ezra excitedly did the math and realized he would need to raise several hundred dollars to host his second party. And instead of becoming dismayed upon seeing the amount, he instead chose to think: "How can I afford this?"

I was impressed that not only did he have several ideas for income, he also understood the need to scale. He brainstormed several ideas, including but not limited to:

- *Run lemonade stands and coach his friends on how to do the same.*

- *Write and sell comic books and coach his friends on how to do the same.*

- *Manufacture wands for adults and children who were into the* Harry Potter *series but needed a cheaper price point than the officially licensed merchandise— and again, coach his friends on how to do the same.*

- *Play the guitar down at the beach for tips and donations and coach his friends on how to do the same.*

Upon weighing his options, Ezra chose to focus on running a weekly lemonade stand in addition to making and selling wands and playing his guitar at the beach.

Within just *one month*, Ezra had the money he needed to host the party he desired. At seven years old.

Was Ezra's party too expensive? That's a trick question—"too expensive" is a limited mindset. Could he afford it? Yes, by simply moving to asking: "How can I afford it?" and sticking to his plan with determination and grit.

They said, "A truly rich man is one whose children run into his arms even though his hands are empty."

— THINK LIFE *is* DIFFERENT

You can do the very same in your own life. What mindset do you need to adopt? What skills do you need to develop? What value do you need to bring to your audience? What solutions do you need to find for people's problems? Who can you serve? What leadership philosophies do you need to cultivate within yourself? Who do you need to *become*?

The truth is, no matter what you want, you can always afford it. If you live in the United States, you are in a free market that has open mobility and trade. You, Ezra, and I have *already won*. Unlike many of the stories I heard (real or not) while growing up in church, you were created to expand, grow, become more, and live in abundance. When you decide to live into that persona, it's not a matter of expense—it's only a matter of time.

THE SHIFT FROM SCARCITY TO ABUNDANCE

I went from being the guy who thought that wanting money and wealth were evil … to a very financially wealthy man. And I haven't lost or sacrificed any part of *myself* to make that change. If anything, I've grown even more into the person I was meant to be. The person I *needed* to be for my clients, my family, and myself.

Over the years, I have learned that on its own, money isn't inherently good or bad—it's simply a tool. It's our use of it, and our intentions with it, that determine its morality. So, if we value our money more than we value people and our relationships, of course we're going to have trouble fitting our metaphorical camel through the eye of that metaphorical needle.

But we can use the tool of money for good, to improve our families' and communities' lives, to give back and to serve, and I'd like to invite you to join me in that amazing place. You were created to expand, grow, and live in abundance. Live into that mindset, cultivate your inner circle, begin to retell your money story, and begin asking, "How can I afford this?"

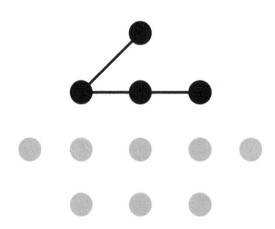

Growth Equals Pain

"Without struggle, there could be no progress."

– FREDERICK DOUGLASS

Remember when you were a child, running wild and free, chasing butterflies? Do you remember that incredible rush of excitement and joy?

I don't know what it is about butterflies that captures our hearts, imaginations, and souls at such a young age, but I can tell you from my own childhood experience that it's powerful. These tiny creatures are beautiful, unique, and awe-inspiring, and their delicate structure and ephemeral nature only add to their mystique.

I remember visiting Pismo Beach, California, one year with my wife and son to watch the migration of the monarch butterflies. There we were, standing on the Earth's crust and looking up into a forest of towering trees … and we didn't see anything. There was nothing there.

Amanda and I had promised our son that he would see one of the most incredible insects with one of the most incredible migration patterns in the world. We had told him stories about how these tiny creatures that weighed less than an ounce would manage to fly three thousand miles just to sleep. We told him about the dangers the monarchs would face from predators trying to slaughter and eat them, and about the unbearable weather conditions, and their fate of certain death … and there was *nothing*.

That's when the tour guide stepped in, and, just like Rafiki from *The Lion King*, encouraged us to "*Loooook harderrrrrr.*" And that's when we suddenly saw them. Thousands of monarch butterflies perched in the trees *en masse*, hiding in plain sight, just as magnificent as promised.

As we stared at those migrating butterflies, many impossible questions came to mind. How were they able to fly so far? How could they triumph over the predators, the weather, and even gravity? How were their thin, delicate wings strong enough to cross three thousand miles, and where does all of their determination come from?

Perhaps the answer awaits us in the story of the monk and the butterfly.

THE MONK AND THE BUTTERFLY

Years ago, in a far-off land, there lived a young monk. Every day, he and his brothers at the monastery would go on a peaceful stroll along their favorite path, passing the same trees, the same stream, and the same landmarks each time. They would even stop to smell the same roses.

One day, the young monk paused and let the elder monks walk ahead so that he could study a cocoon to the side of the path. He had spotted a tiny hole in the side of the cocoon, and through it, a tiny butterfly struggling to emerge. For five minutes, ten minutes, twenty minutes, the young monk sat and watched the butterfly's attempt at rebirth. The butterfly would struggle, get tired, take a break, and get back to struggling all over again. It was difficult to watch, and after a while, the young monk realized that the insect's periods of rest were getting longer and longer.

"I must do something to help my little butterfly friend," he thought, but something inside of him warned him not to interfere with the natural process. The monk continued to watch and wait as the butterfly exhausted itself again and again, fighting what appeared to be a losing battle with survival. He was filled with concern that the butterfly would never emerge and never take to the skies to fulfill its natural destiny.

Finally, he could not take the little creature's suffering anymore and very gently reached out and widened the hole in the cocoon. Soon after, the butterfly emerged, its beautiful, crumpled wings touching the sunlight for the very first time. The young monk watched with joy as the butterfly attempted to spread its wings … and failed. Confused, the monk continued watching as the butterfly repeatedly attempted to spread its wings for flight, only to stumble and remain crumpled on the branch outside of its cocoon. After a while, it tried to jump but failed at that too. After hours of trying in vain to soar into the sky like the rest of its species, the butterfly never fully opened its wings and died right there on the branch, its destiny unfulfilled.

Crushed and confused, the young monk caught up with his elders and explained what had happened. He told them how he had tried to help the butterfly in good faith and kindness—how he had tried to save

They said, "Faith is great, knowledge is great, plans are great, hopes are great, BUT without daily, consistent ACTION, none of them matter. Consistent action, activity, and doing the WORK produces the miracle."

— THINK LIFE *is* DIFFERENT

the little creature from certain doom but how it had met its doom regardless. How could a good deed be met with such a sad ending?

He didn't understand what had happened, just as he didn't understand why the faces of the monks around him were so visibly disappointed. He felt as if he had failed some sort of test or once again performed his *dhutanga practices* in a less than favorable way.

At last, one of the elders told the young monk that, even though he had acted in good faith, he was still responsible for the death of the butterfly. The elder explained that the butterfly gains the strength to unfurl its wings and fly through the struggle it faces while emerging from its cocoon. The struggle is difficult but necessary for the butterfly's survival, and if the process is disrupted, the butterfly will die.

The struggle makes us strong. Without hardship and discomfort, we do not learn and grow. If you rob the butterfly of its opportunity to break through its own barriers, even though the process is painful and hard to watch, you rob it of the strength and endurance it will need later to fulfill its destiny.

These harsh but fair laws of nature apply not only to butterflies but to us as human beings as well.

HEROES AND STRUGGLES

As one of my favorite American heroes, Frederick Douglass, once said, "Without struggle, there could be no progress." Whether we are talking about individuals like Nelson Mandela, Thomas Edison, Anne Frank, the Wright brothers, Michael Jordan, or Jesus, this statement proves itself true time and time again. We see it, too, in movements like women's suffrage, the civil rights movement, the abolition of slavery, and the defeat of Hitler—progress is born of struggle.

Which makes me wonder … why do we expect life to be so easy? Why do we think that we are exempt from suffering and therefore personal development and growth? Why do we complain when faced with obstacles and try to find the detour, the easy path, or the cheat codes around the struggles?

In his book *The Obstacle Is the Way*, author Ryan Holiday confirms Frederick Douglass's statement with the wisdom of the Stoics from centuries before. He notes that life is not inherently easy, nor *should* it be, if you wish to grow, stretch your wings, and do *more* than simply sit on the couch and *exist*.

But, for me at least, this wasn't something I thought about until it was taught to me. Until then, I had lived under the false philosophy that life should be fun and easy. And when things weren't fun and easy, I curled up into a little ball and pouted, hoped, wished, and prayed that my problems would magically go away. What I didn't understand at that time was that by hoping, wishing, and praying that my life would magically get easier, I was really communicating that I wanted my marriage, my businesses, my bank account, my effectiveness, my impact, my value and my purpose to stay stagnant and not grow or change for the better.

In order for that butterfly to build wings strong enough to fly, it needed to first struggle out of that cocoon. Within that struggle is the hidden miracle. Within that struggle is the discovery of our own strength.

THE SEED

Growing up, one of my favorite things to do was watch TV. I know … shocker, right? Maybe the same was true for you as well. But, perhaps surprisingly, my favorite channel was not Nickelodeon, ESPN, BET, or MTV. Nope. My favorite channel was National Geographic. I loved watching life move in and out of form, and I was fascinated by all of the different shapes, sizes, defense mechanisms, weaponry, and behaviors all the creatures in the animal kingdom possessed. I could sit and watch the brute strength of the lions and the entrancing, slow movement of the sloths all day.

In those days, and in my opinion, no one captured the majestic beauty of nature better than Dewitt Jones. To this day, I still remember being absolutely riveted by his still shots and slow-motion filming of plants and animals. One of my most electrifying memories is of watching one of his time-lapse clips of a seed being placed in the ground and erupting into a full-grown plant. I remember thinking, "How can something so small go through such a torturous process?" How could a seed go from being practically *nothing* to *something*?

In my child's mind, watching something go from *nothing* to *something* felt like nothing short of magic. It felt like a miracle. It was a lot like the stories I had heard in Sunday school: a paralyzed man suddenly being able to walk or barrels of water suddenly becoming barrels of wine. How could something all of a sudden *happen* or *exist* like that? I became addicted to finding miracles in real life, and it all started with those time-lapse films.

Today, as an adult, I realize that what I was seeing on TV was simply a sped-up version of a process that took days, weeks, or months to occur in nature. And I got to enjoy watching that process from the comfort of my own home, often in the company of friends, family, and plenty of snacks. But what had Dewitt witnessed? What was the process like for him?

I tried imagining what it must have been like for Dewitt to go to the same place, day after day, hoping, wishing, and praying for change. Watching and waiting, the patience of his human eye a match for the patience of the seed as it painstakingly completed its journey. I wondered what it would be like to experience that kind of patience as the seed traveled from the bird's mouth high in the forest canopy down to the surface of the terrain, as it patiently waited on the Earth's floor for the right amount of wind, rain, sun, and insects to bury and germinate it.

Once underneath the soil, the seed needed to not only fight its way out of its hard outer shell but the tough, thick layer of soil above it as well. Then, if it was going to truly become what it was called to become, it needed to battle insects, heat, fires, drought, contamination, disease, and even other plants. Its struggles would *literally never stop*.

But despite every struggle, with all of the constant pain, frustrations, obstacles, and disasters, this simple little seed battled through, moving unfailingly toward its focus—the sun. And after several hundred years, the giant redwood tree, now at its full splendor and potential, would look back on its seedling days with gratitude and think, "Wow! Growth sure does result from pain. Without all of those struggles I faced, I never could have progressed to this amazing level."

Like a seed biding its time beneath the soil, our thoughts, lives, ideas, businesses, marriages, and callings need us to stay strong, focus on the light, and keep fighting until one day we, too, reach our full potential.

CAN SOMEONE PLEASE HAVE THIS BABY FOR ME?

February 25, 2011 was the day the biggest miracle of my young life took place—it was the day our first child, Ezra, was born. It was a surreal experience, and I remember it so vividly to this day that I feel like a time traveler, able to experience it over and over again at will. From the moment of his delivery, there was no denying that Ezra was my child. It was like looking at my own head, face, shoulders, back, and butt … just on a smaller frame. I mean, this child was my identical twin. All that I am and all that I'll ever be was birthed on the same day as Ezra.

My wife, needless to say, had a very different birthing experience than I did. The pregnancy was remarkably different for each of us as well. For me, it was an interesting study of my wife's behaviors in response to her condition. But for Amanda, it was a trial of sickness and suffering.

The morning sickness of the first trimester was a doozy. Amanda suffered bouts of sickness that would stop her dead in her tracks. We'd make plans to hang out with friends and have to cancel at the last minute because she would suddenly become bedridden. We would go out to eat, and a bite or even the smell of the wrong food would trigger a complete physical breakdown.

The second and third trimesters brought nausea, hot flashes, and more illness triggers, from smells to even sitting in the car for too long. Her sleep was fragmented, and she was constantly in a state of discomfort. I could always tell if she was going to have a good day or a bad day based on the number of water bottles she had on hand. If she wasn't feeling well, she would grab a water bottle, pour some water into her hand, and gently wipe it on her face.

She did this over and over and over again, enduring morning sickness, afternoon sickness, and night sickness throughout the duration of the pregnancy. As Ezra continued to expand and take up more space, she would rub her belly from morning until night. Consciously or subconsciously, her hands and arms were in constant movement as she sought in desperation to ease the intense feelings of discomfort.

My wife's experience is not unique to her; millions of women go through the exact same thing. In fact, many of the women reading this might have been triggered by the events described above, especially from my young, dumb, and lacking-in-empathy male perspective. How could I know what it's like to experience the real-life feelings and dealings of motherhood and the pain and patience it takes to carry a child inside one's body for nine months? Who am I to speak in such a cavalier fashion about a process I know nothing about?

To be honest, I don't know, and I can't. So, let me get right to the point of my message before I get into any more trouble. If you ran into a woman, and she said any of the following statements, what would you think?

- *"I want to have the baby, but I don't want to deal with the discomfort of pregnancy."*
- *"I want to have the baby, but I don't want the morning sickness."*
- *"I want to have the baby, but I don't want my sleep disturbed."*
- *"I want to have the baby, but I don't want to miss out on any fun activities."*
- *"I want to have the baby, but I don't want to feel tired."*
- *"I want to have the baby, but I don't want to feel pain."*
- *"I want to have the baby, but I don't want to gain weight."*
- *"I want to have the baby, but I don't want the stretch marks."*
- *"I want to have the baby, but I don't want to grow or change at all."*

It's understandable not to want any of the side effects from pregnancy, but it's not incredibly realistic. In fact, a woman who says one or more of these statements might be downright delusional. You can't pick and choose what you want about the process—you take the entire experience as a package deal.

They said, "Losing weight and becoming exceedingly wealthy take the same mental discipline, habits, and self-control. Do what most won't do now, so that later, you can live like most can't."

— THINK LIFE *is* DIFFERENT

Everyone knows that having a baby comes with nausea, sleepless nights, weight gain, frustration, and stretch marks. Without those struggles, there is no miracle. If you reject the pain of the process, then you reject the growth that it brings. And this doesn't just apply to literal childbirth. If you're going to birth *anything* in life—a new idea, a business, a product, a lasting marriage, etc.—it has to go through a gestational period, and that period will more often than not bring its own share of discomfort and pain.

You cannot birth new life without going through some kind of discomfort or pain. Without struggle, there can be no progress.

MUSCLES ALWAYS TELL THE TRUTH

When I was fifteen years old, pretty much the only thing that could motivate me was sports. If all I ever achieved in life was that football scholarship, that would have been enough for me. I wanted so badly to be like Warrick Dunn and the other athletes I saw on television. Night and day, all I thought about was playing ball … but there was a big problem.

I didn't think I was very good.

Baseball, yes—I had put in my 1,095,000 swings and dedicated myself fully to the craft. But football … not so much. You see, up until my sophomore year in high school, I had always been on the "husky" side. I didn't get my clothes from the "normal" brand-name stores like my friends did; nope, I shopped at the Big & Tall store. If and when I did go to one of those "normal" stores, I had to travel past all of the "normal" aisles to the back, where the Big & Tall section was located.

Even after I lost all of my excess weight, I still didn't look like the other kids at my school, and I *definitely* didn't look like the other football players. Even though I was fast, I was weirdly scrawny and had *zero* muscle mass. And while I had played football in years prior, I had only played the offensive or defensive line.

But as a sophomore in high school, I was invited by the head football coach to join the varsity football team.

My response was, "Wait, what? Me?!" I simply couldn't believe it. "Did Coach make a mistake?" I asked, feeling the need to double check. "Is he sure he wants me to play *varsity*?" It made absolutely no sense, and to this day, all I can assume is that the head coach must have seen something in me that I did not.

The thought of playing on the field with the other men who looked like *actual football players*—mythical, Herculean figures rippling with well-developed muscles—was terrifying. I feared that if I got tackled by one of those monstrous dudes, I would die. I was so scared, nervous, and unsure of myself. If only my body were mature like everyone else's, I thought. If only I had a physique like Christian Okoye. If only I had big muscles like the juniors and seniors on the varsity team … then I could be great.

I remember wanting to have muscles at that time in my life. But I also remember not wanting to put in the hard work to build them. Does that make sense? I had the desire to *look* like a powerful, dominant football player, but the desire to push through the time, discomfort, and effort to get my body there was severely lacking. I wanted muscles, but only if it came easy. So basically, I stayed the same.

I finished out my sophomore, junior, and senior seasons on the varsity team and headed off to college—and surprisingly, I *did* get that college football scholarship that I had craved for years and years. But I wasn't as proud of it as I wanted to be. Because I still didn't think I was very good.

I had progressed on the field by relying solely on my natural, God-given abilities. I got by with my speed and elusiveness; I could run past and around everyone. Rarely did I need to run *through* anyone, and, because I didn't need to do it, I didn't. I still wasn't putting in the time or effort to lift weights and build up my body because it was easier not to, and I saw no real need for it.

We make the decision to change when the pain of staying the same outweighs the pain of changing, and at that time, there was no pain in staying the same. What I was doing was working. I could still score several touchdowns and run for hundreds of yards. My desire for those muscles wasn't strong enough to overcome my distaste for lifting.

Then things changed. Going into my senior year in college, I found that the university had begun recruiting some really stellar young talent. These boys were bigger, faster, and stronger than me, and I made the late-in-the-game realization that it was possible one of them might take my starting position. Maybe I was fast enough, but no way was I strong enough to compete with them.

That summer, I started researching past and present professional athletes like Olympic 200-meter and 400-meter gold medalist Michael Johnson, NBA Hall of Famer David Robinson, NFL All-Pro Ed Reed, and more. I became obsessed with their workout routines and marveled at how fiercely they attacked the gym. I wanted to understand how they both built strength and maintained their natural speed and stamina.

Finally, I stumbled across an old recording of boxing legend Muhammad Ali. He was speaking about his work ethic, his strength, and how he had put on so much muscle mass over the years. One of the interviewers asked him, "When you work out, how many reps do you do?"

His response was legendary: "I'm not sure. I don't start counting until it starts to hurt."

The incredible thing about building up muscle mass is that it's actually very easy to do. The challenge is that it's just easier *not to* do it. What do I mean? Well, let's say you wanted to build up your biceps. In order to build those muscles, you would need to push them past their maximum capacity, which means literally tearing them down.

Muscle tissue grows by tearing and healing over and over, and this process doesn't happen until we are close to failure, that moment at which great trainers will say, "Just one more rep!" and push you to keep going, literally past your breaking point. They try to inspire you to push through the pain to lift the weight just one more time so the muscle can rip just a little bit more and grow back even bigger and stronger. Without the pain, discomfort, failing, and breaking, we don't build those new biceps. Kind of cool, right?

I was terrified of losing my starting position, and that's when the big surround-sound voice kicked in: "If you want to grow those big muscles,

Jamil, you'd better get ready for some discomfort." I knew it was right, and at that time, the pain of losing my prized position on the team outweighed the pain of hitting the gym.

That summer going into my senior year of college football, I went from being able to bench press 225 pounds six or seven times to being able to do it nineteen times. For years I had wanted to get strong and build muscle, but I hadn't wanted to go through the pain of the change. Not until it became absolutely necessary, and the loss of my starting position was threatened, did I decide it was time to build that muscle. But I committed and did it, because without struggle, there can be no progress.

BE WILLING TO LOSE YOUR TAIL

I heard a story once about an incredible group of tailless monkeys called *Barbary macaques* at the Rock of Gibraltar in Spain. Millions of people flock to this historic landmark every year for the chance to interact with one of these four-legged, tailless creatures. And though they live in Spain, science suggests that these monkeys actually originated in the northern part of Africa—Morocco, to be exact—where the monkey population has tails.

Here's a simplified version of what happened. During the Pliocene era, the monkeys lived on the single body of land that today makes up Europe and Africa. As it began to break apart over time, the pieces of land drifted away from each other, splitting the monkeys. Some of the monkeys ended up in what is now southern Spain, at the Rock of Gibraltar, while the rest made their home in northern Africa.

When those monkeys originally landed in Gibraltar, they actually had tails too. Those tails were helpful for balance and safety and often acted as a fifth limb. But because of the tougher climate, unbearable terrain, and freezing temperatures, their tails began to fall off. Yes, you read that right! Here's where it gets even better:

Over a long period of time—some say millions of years—of tails falling off, the monkeys began to evolve to a point where baby Barbary

They promised,
"The obstacle is the way."

— THINK LIFE *is* DIFFERENT

macaques were born with no tails at all. Their species had adapted so well to the pain, discomfort, and struggle that they literally changed their own biology. In order for them to grow, stay relevant, and exist for millions of years, they needed to make some drastic changes, embrace discomfort, and grow strong.

Moral of the story? If you desire to grow, be prepared to lose your tail.

IT HURTS, DOESN'T IT?

When I first began building our business, I admittedly had no idea what I was doing. In a way, I felt like a refugee who had been relocated to a foreign land; I felt lost and afraid, but I wanted a better life so badly it didn't matter.

I woke up every morning obsessed with becoming successful and providing value. I lost sleep dreaming about my goals and all of the things I wanted to accomplish. I had spoken to mentors and successful business owners and knew that my new venture could produce incredible fruit. I had been inspired by a vision of what was possible, and I could not shake it.

The only problem was … I didn't know how to do it.

After I quit my full-time job to focus solely on building my business, things picked up a bit. My laser focus and efforts allowed me to attract more clients and begin to find new business partners, which initially led to a quick flash of success. Friends on the sidelines tell me it looked like we "shot out of the gate," but it never felt that way to me.

My vision, my ambition, and my appetite for success were huge, and all I ever felt was this overwhelming sense that nothing was happening—or, if things were happening, they were certainly not happening quickly enough.

Ten months into the business, my business partners and I hit a major milestone, and we decided to celebrate. We gave out plaques and awards, snagged speaking opportunities, and enjoyed a spike in revenue as well as more liquidity. After ten months of pushing, scratching, and clawing, I finally allowed myself to feel a tiny bit of success.

My business partners were happy. The business's overall momentum seemed to be flowing smoothly, more value was being provided to the marketplace, and even my marriage began to improve. But success comes and goes like a thief in the night, and our happiness was short-lived.

The business very quickly and unexpectedly started to decline. Partners who had promised their loyalty and sworn that they were in it for the long haul began to leave without any explanation. Revenue stopped increasing, and we were no longer able to attract the top-tier talent. I stopped giving talks onstage of "How We Did It" and began to watch my business—and my confidence—plummet like the stock market crash of 1929.

At that time, I felt like Dr. Martin Luther King, Jr. when he gave his famous "I've Been to the Mountaintop" speech in Memphis, Tennessee. I had been to the mountaintop, and I feared I would never reach it again. I stayed up day and night trying to figure out how to turn things back around, how to right the wrongs, and how to puzzle out what the wrongs even *were*. I tried to figure out what had been said and done and why folks who had appeared happy would just up and leave.

I couldn't make any sense of it. I wanted to find the solution, but it was playing "Where's Waldo" with me. I tried different training techniques, hosted more meetings, called more people, encouraged my team more frequently, tried to revive a spark of passion in those who had left, attempted new innovations, attended more seminars, and consulted everyone in the industry I knew who I thought might be able to help me.

But nothing helped, and my business continued to fail.

At that point, I was no longer chasing that light, that vision of success. At that point, I simply wanted the hurt, pain, and frustration to go away. I was desperate to know why this was happening—and why it was happening to *me*! I was working harder than ever and doing everything I possibly could to save my business. I was following all of the advice my esteemed colleagues and mentors had shared with me. But nothing was helping.

I found myself saying and thinking things like:

- *"Why is there no growth?!"*

- *"Why are we not seeing results?!"*

- *"Why aren't our clients and business partners doing what they said they wanted to do?!"*

- *"Why am I spending so much time implementing new strategies, with no evidence they are working?!"*

- *"Why am I not meeting my goals?!"*

- *"Is my life going to stay like this forever?!"*

A few months into the decline, I attended a seminar in Nashville, Tennessee. I knew going in that there was only one reason I was going: a certain woman was going to be in attendance, and *I knew she could help me.*

She was a prominent figure in the industry who had built an incredible business in a relatively short span of time. She was known as a master innovator and motivator and had a reputation for helping people like me experience massive shifts to reach their peak potential.

I knew I had to talk to her. I craved what she had and wanted to emulate the business and success that she had. With my intentions in place, I traveled to the conference and began my search.

On day one, she was nowhere to be found. On day two, nope … didn't see her. Finally, on day three, I spotted her like a cheetah spotting a gazelle. *There she is, over by the courtyard, and she's walking alone,* I thought gleefully. *Now's my chance!* Usually when I saw her, she had a crowd around her like she was John Lennon, but this time, it was like God had ordained a divine meeting. I beelined toward her and, frantic as a little boy who'd had his lunch money stolen, told her my story.

It poured out like verbal vomit—how my business was crumbling, how my partners were leaving, how my revenue was declining and my liquidity vanishing. I hit her with everything that had been building up in my brain, all of my issues and stressors in an encyclopedic torrent that left no detail unexplained and no emotion unfelt. I swear, if it was possible to win an Academy Award for dumping all over someone, they would have called me Denzel Washington that day.

Her response? "It hurts, doesn't it?"

Yeah. That was her response to the Golden Globe-winning, Oscar-nominated, Grammy-obtaining song and dance I had just laid on her. I blinked—I had never been so upset, confused, and disappointed all at once like that in my entire life.

The conversation continued:

Me: "What the hell does that mean?"

Her: "Your desire is to be successful, right? To build something incredible?"

Me: "Yes."

Her: "Well, you're in it. You're in it right now. You're in the process."

Me: "What?"

Her: "This hurt. This pain. This frustration that you're feeling right now … it's all part of the process of getting to where you want to be and becoming what you want to become."

Me: "… I don't get it."

Her: "Just keep feeling this hurt, keep feeling this pain, and keep asking these questions. Eventually, it'll all make sense."

And then she walked away.

I had honestly never been so upset at one person in my life as I was with her that day. In my head, this was going to be *The Conversation*—the magic bullet that cut through the long, frustrating nights of me wondering where everything had gone wrong. She was supposed to have given me the antitoxin, told me exactly what to do to fix my situation, injected me with some kind of truth serum so that I didn't have to go another day married to discouragement and disappointment.

She was supposed to have fixed my problem. And instead *she had walked away.*

Several months later, as my business continued to decline, I was invited to a prestigious leadership conference. I showed up at that conference full of ego, frustration, shame, and blame. I felt ornery, angry, and like an enormous failure. Six months of daily self-doubt had made my house its home, and I was in full "if only" mode.

If only more people had helped me, mentored me, and shown me the way, then I'd be closer to my goals. If only my wife had as much passion about this business as I had, then I'd be closer to my goals. If only our business partners had not abandoned us, then I would be closer to my goals.

Needless to say, I was a total wreck, but I was desperate enough to keep my mind open to learning and hearing new things. Some old part of Jamil kicked in, and I spent most of the conference listening closely and studying the words and ideas of the speakers. I was hungry—starving, in fact—to be like them.

After a while, I noticed that every speaker and every trainer, at some point in their talk, spoke about how much they read. It was a common theme. They all referenced book after book, noting how reading these materials had helped them in their sales, management, and leadership positions. One woman even said, "Those who don't read are no better off than those who *can't* read."

Whoa! That was mind-blowing to me. At the time, I was not a reader. I was a sports talk-radio listener and a TV watcher, but I was definitely not a reader. I made a promise that day that I would become a voracious reader. I had been looking for the missing puzzle pieces, and this was the first of many that I discovered.

I left the conference with a heavy-hearted and full-blown realization that I had not been acting like a leader. I had not been a leader as a husband, father, friend, business owner, or anything else. I knew that I didn't need to go work on all the things "out there" anymore and that the blame didn't lie with my coaches, mentors, wife, business partners, or anyone else but *me.*

I realized I needed to stop wishing that others would change and start learning how to change myself. Upon leaving the conference, I purchased somewhere between forty and fifty books, all on the topics of leadership, management, spirituality, finance, communication, religion, and entrepreneurship. And within three months, I had read, listened to, or at least spent time with every single one.

I began to discover personal development speakers that connected with my heart and soul. I began to attract new business partners who were more in line with my vision and mission. Slowly, I began to see that there was light at the end of the tunnel.

WHEN IT ALL MAKES SENSE

The shift came this time in a hotel room in Pismo Beach, California. It was a cold night, and the waves were crashing loudly against the beach outside. My wife and son were lying next to me when it hit me … growth equals pain.

Suddenly, it all made sense. After all those months of long nights spent worrying, after all of those intense conversations with others and myself, after all of the ups and downs, the questioning of my own ability and sanity, and wondering if business-building was really for me … it finally hit me. I finally understood what that woman back in Nashville had been trying to tell me.

Everything I had just been through—all of that pain and suffering and anxiety—was part of the process. It *had* to happen that way. It had to be hard. It had to be painful. Without the pain, how could I learn the lessons? Without the pain, what would drive and pressure me to change?

Without pain, how else could I build my strength and endurance? Without experiencing loss, how else could I be the leader of thousands? Without experiencing difficulty, how else could I understand how to navigate difficult situations? Without doubting myself, how else could I build confidence?

I couldn't mentor, teach, or coach someone else to handle something I wasn't strong enough to handle myself. I couldn't build something

They said, "It's the
journey that's important,
not the destination."

— THINK LIFE *is* DIFFERENT

sustainable and long-lasting on a foundation of quicksand. I couldn't fully understand my own capabilities without an obstacle.

As I lay there, gently chuckling to myself, I remembered the words of one of the great leaders I had just read about: Frederick Douglass, whom I still quote to this day. "Without struggle," he famously said, "there could be no progress."

A week later, I got those words tattooed on my right forearm so that I would never forget where I had come from.

From that moment on, in that little hotel room off the coast of California, I adopted a new philosophy. Instead of running away from the hard things, and instead of moaning and groaning about them, I would begin embracing them. I had just read Ryan Holiday's legendary book *The Obstacle Is the Way* for the first time, and its message had resonated with me in a big way.

That second year of my business was the hardest year I'd ever had, but I was and continue to be grateful for it. It made me stronger, wiser, and better, and best of all, it made me prove to myself that if I ever faced hard times again, I'd be able to handle it.

Success is rented, my friends, and that rent is due every day. Success is never free. It always comes with a price and will always require growth, which we now know requires pain and discomfort in turn. As the great Jim Rohn once said, that life can be summed up like this: "Opportunity mixed with difficulty." So, whether the butterfly, our heroes, the mother, your muscles, tailless monkeys, or myself as I built my business, if we focus on avoiding struggle we can miss opportunities for progress.

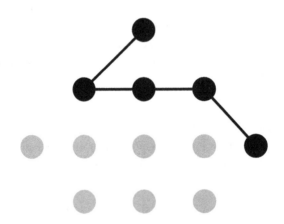

Shift Five

Light Yourself on Fire

"You are an ace. Light yourself on fire."

– KIM FISKE

In 1999, the legendary film *The Matrix* debuted and captivated audiences around the world. It was full of action, drama, and stunts that, thanks to 21st century graphics, were not humanly possible. My buddy and I raced to a movie theater in Alhambra, California, to see what all the hype was about—the entire school was buzzing, and we didn't want to be left out.

For those of you who have never seen the movie, here's a brief synopsis: A man named Morpheus, played by Laurence Fishburne, is the leader of the free world in the aftermath of a robot uprising and apocalypse. The humans lost the war, and part of Morpheus's mission is to find the one person who can lead them Moses-like out of bondage and despair. Appropriately, this person is called "the One," and Morpheus has been told by an oracle that he is destined to find him.

After years of searching, Morpheus finds a young man named Neo, played by Keanu Reeves. Neo is a regular guy with a regular desk job who just happens to be searching for a larger calling in his life. Soon, he faces a tug-of-war between choosing normalcy and greatness. He makes the decision to take a symbolic red pill that will free his mind from the grasp of the Matrix and allow him to lead humanity to freedom. He chooses to become *the One.*

Throughout the film, although Neo has on a surface level accepted that he is the One, he never really *believes* or internalizes it. He is plagued with constant self-doubt and feelings that he could not possibly be *enough* to save everyone. Each fight and each confrontation with the enemy gives him yet another piece of evidence that Morpheus might be right, that he might be the One, and he takes one step closer to believing.

Finally, Neo stands toe-to-toe with the film's bad guy in an epic climax, and he has finally reached the point where he's not hoping he's the One or even merely believing he's the One—he *knows* that he is. And with that knowledge, the fight slows down, leaving Neo in total control to shape the situation as he wishes.

Over the years I've thought a lot about that movie and asked myself, "Why didn't Neo just trust Morpheus from the very beginning?

They said, "Not everyone
is going to get it.
Do it anyway."

— THINK LIFE *is* DIFFERENT

Why did it take him going through all of those fights, disappointments, failures, and disbelief? Why was it so hard for him to believe?"

I've since realized that, when I ask those questions about Neo, what I'm doing is really asking those questions about *myself*. You see, when I first started building our business, I was absolutely blessed to have multiple Morpheus-like figures in my life. These guides, mentors, and coaches told me that I had greatness within me but, like Neo, I didn't quite believe them. I had to go through a difficult and challenging learning period to move from accepting to believing to *knowing*.

So, what does it take to fully *know* your greatness and to be truly successful in any area you want?

STUDYING OPRAH

In 2013 and 2014, I became obsessed with studying Oprah's interview style and technique. Day and night, I watched YouTube videos of her, studying how she acted and reacted through her voice and body language, leaning in, shifting her tone, changing the inflection of her voice, and more.

One of my favorite moments was during Oprah's interview with John F. Kennedy, Jr. Before the interview, John had requested that they not speak about his mother, Jackie Kennedy Onassis, or his father, John F. Kennedy. Yet Oprah knew that, in order for her audience to get the full and true essence of his heart, she would need to encourage him to do just that.

During the interview, she skillfully led him toward the topic of his parents, and it was clear that John knew what she was doing. Oprah sensed that John was growing uneasy and began to do something that only she could do so well—she began to tell his story through *her* own life experience of hurt, pain, tragedy, and disappointment. She leaned in toward him more and more with each story, and after a while, he leaned in, too, and allowed her to lead him into that deeply personal space he had not wanted to enter.

In that moment, I knew I had cracked part of the code that would lead me to the success I wanted. I would need to emulate Oprah and practice what the Buddhists call "deep listening," which is the art of moving from listening to understanding through the asking of artful questions.

Three interviews truly stood out to me, and I'd like to share with you what I learned from them now. These were Oprah's interviews with Pharrell Williams, J.K. Rowling, and Thich Nhat Hanh.

PHARRELL WILLIAMS

Pharrell Williams is a great American rapper, singer, songwriter, record producer, entrepreneur, and fashion designer, whose song "Happy" went viral in the US and UK in 2014. It gave me goosebumps to see these two iconic leaders—Oprah and Pharrell—seated together for their interview. Pharrell sat there with a posh money-green top hat that screamed a complete comfort in his being-ness, and Oprah sat in a subdued pale-yellow jacket and gray pants, a study in casual confidence.

During the interview, Oprah took the audience through the journey of Pharrell's life, from his early days of growing up biracial Black and white in the projects of one of Virginia's inner cities to exploring music at a young age and realizing he had a special gift.

Pharrell's relationship with music fascinated me; I had never heard anyone talk about it before in the way that he did. He said that he didn't see the world around him in substance or form like most people did. Instead, he saw everything in colors and melodies. For him, everything was music. And, as he would later learn, the music was *him*.

For Pharrell, the process of *becoming* and then *being* this person was one full of questions and doubt. He constantly doubted himself, his purpose, his decisions, his friendships, and even his *being*, all while asking, "Why me?"

The shift came when Pharrell consciously realized the difference between *doing* and *being*. He wasn't *doing* music; he *was* the music.

They said, "The book that you won't read won't help."

— THINK LIFE *is* DIFFERENT

He wasn't *doing* producing; he was producing *in ecstatic motion*. He wasn't creating; he was *part of the creator*.

During the interview, Oprah played a video segment of hundreds of people in different countries around the world dancing and lip-syncing to "Happy," and Pharrell breaks down into tears. I think it was right then and there that he moved from the space of questioning, hoping, praying, and merely believing to fully *knowing* that he was, like Neo, "the One."

In this moment, he finally and fully understood that he was a vessel, a vehicle, an instrument that the universe was using to dramatically impact the lives of others. In this intense moment, Pharrell became present and fully aware of his *knowingness*. The moment he moved from believing to knowing, he stopped trying to *do* and let himself *be done*. It's a beautiful moment, and whenever I rewatch it, to this day, I still cry.

J.K. ROWLING

The interview between Oprah and J.K. Rowling (the British novelist and creator of the *Harry Potter* fantasy series) always makes me feel good. I don't know if it's J.K.'s girl-next-door qualities or English charm, or how much I relate to her story, but I feel like I could curl up into a little ball next to the fireplace and just listen to them talk forever.

During the interview, Oprah expertly guides J.K. Rowling down the yellow brick road of her past life, touching on J.K.'s failed first marriage, her time as a single mother living on welfare, her clinical depression, and her years of healing. In every stage, Oprah asks about the lessons she learned, and for each one, J.K. talks about moving from a state of wishing to a state of hoping, to believing, and to *knowing*.

In the grand finale moment of the interview, Oprah plays a clip of J.K.'s commencement address to the Harvard graduating class of 2008, and her words resonate in a beautiful moment of clarity:

> So why do I talk about the benefits of failure? Sim-
> ply because failure meant a stripping away of the inessential.
> I stopped pretending to myself that I was anything other
> than what I was and began to direct all my energy into

finishing the only work that mattered to me. Had I really succeeded at anything else, I might never have found the determination to succeed in the one arena I believed I truly belonged. I was set free because my greatest fear had been realised, and I was still alive, and I still had a daughter whom I adored, and I had an old typewriter and a big idea. And so rock bottom became the solid foundation on which I rebuilt my life.

You might never fail on the scale I did, but some failure in life is inevitable. It is impossible to live without failing at something, unless you live so cautiously that you might as well not have lived at all—in which case, you fail by default.

J.K. had her Neo moment when she finally realized that she was "the One"—that she wasn't put on this Earth to be normal, but to be extraordinary. Even with all of her flaws and failures, she was still perfect and still vibrantly alive. Like Pharrell, she realized she was being used as a vessel, a vehicle, an instrument that the universe was using to dramatically impact the lives of others. And like Pharrell, she stopped trying to *do* and allowed herself to be *done*.

One of Oprah's final questions to J.K. was about happiness, specifically pertaining to the scene in the *Harry Potter* series where Dumbledore talks to Harry about the Mirror of Erised. The magical mirror shows the deepest, most desperate longing of one's heart, and, according to Dumbledore: "The happiest man on earth would be able to use the Mirror of Erised like a normal mirror, that is, he would look into it and see himself exactly as he is."

The happiest man and woman alive are the ones who recognize, understand, and *know* that they are truly "the One," meant to do great and amazing things.

THICH NHAT HANH

When I first caught a glimpse of "Thầy" (as those who know him best refer to him), I was in the rebuilding stages of both my business and my marriage. Despite my massive drive, discipline, and desire, I still didn't have the success that I wanted, and I was having trouble understanding why.

I had studied Buddhism in college for a major world religions course years prior, and one line in particular by the poet Rumi had stuck with me:

The breezes at dawn have secrets to tell you.

Don't go back to sleep.

You must ask for what you really want.

Don't go back to sleep.

With these words ringing in my ears, I lay awake at 3:15 a.m. several mornings in a row, fighting off stress, anxiety, and the wild hope that I could find answers and healing.

Finally, it drove me crazy enough that I started doing a little more research into what this could mean, and YouTube video after YouTube video finally led me to an interview of Oprah with a tiny, oddly dressed man. Curious, I clicked *Play* and then wept as my world was changed forever.

This man was, of course, Thich Nhat Hanh or "Thầy", the Vietnamese Buddhist monk and peace activist, who has published over one hundred books and founded the Plum Village Tradition. His interview with Oprah was the simplest and yet the most profound of them all, and it finally cracked the last piece of the code for me.

As I soaked in Thầy's words, it did not take long for me to begin to understand what was missing from my life, my business, and my marriage—*compassion*. Thầy emanated an overwhelming power of gentleness and loving warmth that felt healing to watch. He was present, calm, conscious, and somehow seemed to operate on a higher frequency than anyone else I had seen.

In his interview, Thầy shared a series of four mantras that he used whenever he felt triggered, out of alignment, or upset. I have adopted these mantras as my own in my daily search for mindful living and compassion in relationships:

They said, "The morning breeze has something to tell you. Don't go back to sleep ... Don't go back to sleep ..."

— THINK LIFE *is* DIFFERENT

1. *"Darling, I'm here for you."*

2. *"Darling, I know you are there, and I am so happy."*

3. *"Darling, I know you're suffering. That is why I am here for you."*

4. *"Darling, I suffer. I am trying my best to practice. Please help me."*

These four mantras serve to offer others and yourself the gift of your presence, which can be in turn used to alleviate suffering and share healing, compassion, and love.

When Thầy was seven-years-old, he saw the Buddha for the first time and fell in love with the figure's peaceful, smiling presence. He decided that he wanted to serve as that presence for other people, and when he turned sixteen, his parents granted him permission to become ordained as a Buddhist monk.

When Oprah asked how Thầy could possibly have known he wanted to be a monk at such a young age, he responded: "I would not be happy if I could not become a monk. They call it the beginner's mind—the deep intention, the deepest desire that a person may have. And I can say that until this day, this beginner's mind is still alive in me."

Several years after joining the monastery, war broke out in Thầy's home country of Vietnam. After doing his duty of speaking out against the war, Thầy was banished and exiled from his home for nearly forty years. But even in exile, Thầy continued to move from hoping, wishing, and believing to *knowing* that he was being used as a vessel, a vehicle, an instrument that the universe was using to dramatically impact the lives of others. Like Neo, he knew all along that there was something bigger out there and took action to become "the One."

LIGHT YOURSELF ON FIRE

As I continued down the hungry, desperate path toward success, I spent a lot of time getting mentally, emotionally, and psychologically kicked in the face. The abuse seemed constant, and I couldn't for the life of me figure out what I had done to deserve it. I didn't know why my business, relationships, and finances were not growing—or, as it felt at the time, *actively fleeing* in the opposite direction.

A good friend and mentor took pity on my struggling self and set up a time for me to have a one-on-one with one of the best and brightest minds in my industry, Kim Fiske. The commute to have this conversation would be two hours each way, but truthfully, I would have driven to the other side of the planet to get answers.

I arrived in San Diego and limped into the hotel restaurant a battered and broken man. And there she was, sitting in the middle of the crowd, a fiery beacon of hope who I almost dared not approach. I was nervous to meet with her, but desperation finally overrode my timidity, and I sat down at her table.

She greeted me by asking, "What do you want out of life?"

Immediately, the dam broke, and I began to verbally spew my aspirations, my hopes, my prayers, my dreams that things would change … and my frustration about how it was *simply not happening*. I was doing everything that everyone had told me to do, but I wasn't getting the results. Change seemed to be out of my reach.

And then it happened. I received the final two numbers I had needed to open the combination lock to all of the answers I had been seeking.

In essence, Kim told me: "Success is not something you chase after and try to acquire. No, no, no. Success is something you attract by becoming an attractive person. Your energy, your beliefs, your knowingness—they're all on a frequency that is way down here." She gestured toward the floor with her hand. "And you're trying to attract something and accomplish something that's way up here." With that, she gestured toward the ceiling and continued.

"You need to light yourself on fire, young man, and have your flame shine *so bright* that others cannot help but keep their eyes on you. How many cards are there in a deck? That's right—fifty-two. And how many aces are there within those fifty-two cards? Exactly—only four. *You are an ace.*"

For some reason, it finally clicked. That's how I got my last two numbers to the combination lock of success. Up until that moment, I had been like Pharrell, a little boy in the projects of Virginia who didn't yet see the music in himself. I had been like J.K. Rowling, standing on the rock of pain and ready to rebuild my life. I had been like Thầy, exiled from the home and compassion he had known and determined to recreate it for himself in his heart.

Up until that moment, I had been really only hoping, wishing, and praying for things to change. For things to *be*. But I hadn't *internalized* it. I hadn't made it part of my *identity*. I hadn't recognized myself *as* success. I hadn't *known* myself to be the thing I had been searching for all along.

I had walked around for years thinking I was a jack of spades, failing to realize that I was an ace. That I was "the One." That I already had inside of me everything I needed and desired. That I didn't need to *do*— that I simply needed to be *done*. All that time, I hadn't known that I only had to move from accepting to believing to *knowing* I was "the One," an ace, and that from there, I could manifest everything I needed.

Once you move from believing to knowing, you will become unstoppable, and it is another superpower that you possess.

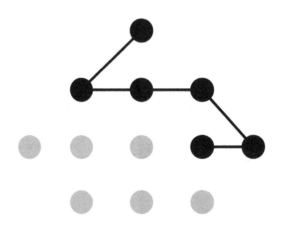

Shift Six

Fear Is Rocket Fuel

"Your playing small doesn't serve the world."

– MARIANNE WILLIAMSON

Most of my life tends to pass by in a blur as I work on my business, write and respond to emails, do chores around the house, and spend time with my kids. But for many of us, there are certain dates in history that have crystallized in our memories—certain days we will never forget.

For some, it's the assassination of a leader like John F. Kennedy or Martin Luther King, Jr. For others, it's a remarkable event, like the moon landing, the day of the Pearl Harbor attack, or the day that the Twin Towers came crashing down in New York City.

On these days, we tend to remember where we were and what we were doing with remarkable clarity, as step by step the unforgettable events unfolded in real time. Decades later, we are able to recount where we were at the precise time of the event, as well as what we were wearing, who we were with, and even the smell in the air. We remember adjacent things, too, like a lecture a professor taught earlier that day or a song that was playing on the radio.

I've spoken to people who remember the day the Civil Rights Act of 1964 was passed, and even though it was over fifty years later, their emotions still came stampeding back as powerfully as a herd of buffalo. The joy, the sorrow, the hurt, the pain, the grief, the relief, the calmness, and the fear—it all came rushing back, alive as it had been on the day it had happened.

For me, the date I will never forget is March 3, 1991. I was ten-years-old and making my way through the dog days of the fifth grade. We had just moved from a predominantly Black neighborhood and school district to a largely white neighborhood and school district, and, as maybe one of fifteen Black kids in the entire school, I was still trying to figure out my place and my identity in the world.

It was a complete culture shock, but after a while I learned how to assimilate. From the shoes I wore to the style of my hair and even the video games I played, I slowly began to fit in. Now, around my Black friends and family, you wouldn't catch me dead wearing Vans, watching MTV, listening to Vanilla Ice, or buying clothes from Anchor Blue. Around them, I reverted back to the self they had always known me to be. It created a strange duality, a need to begin code-switching between the two cultures I inhabited.

Finally, on March 3, 1991, it happened. We were sitting at home as a family on Acaso Drive, watching our black-and-white television set, when the news broke: "We have gotten reports that a man was brutally beaten by police officers in Los Angeles, California, and has been taken into custody. We believe his name to be Rodney King."

It seemed like the videos and images flashed across the scene for hours—a Black man being beaten by white cops, caught on camera by a bystander. Evidence of injustice inherent in a broken system, being talked about everywhere, from barbershops to family cookouts to every home with a television set.

This event marked the first time I ever remember being *truly afraid* in life.

The thought of heading into my all-white school after witnessing the reports of this event was uncomfortable at best. I found myself wondering: Would I be able to pick sides between my white friends and Black family members if push came to shove? Could I face the pressure, real or imagined? Could I really trust my newfound white friends? What would the police do if they found *me*?

I remember walking to school as a ten-year-old Black boy eyeing the bushes and wondering if someone would jump out and assault me. I became terrified of police cars and white police officers and winced when they passed me by on the street. I took the long way to school through side streets and out-of-the-way neighborhoods to decrease my chances of spotting the "po-po."

I knew for a fact that I was next, and no one could convince me otherwise. That violent beating I had witnessed haunted my nightmares and my daydreams. Rodney's fate would be mine, whether in school or out in the streets. I knew it was coming. The fear said it was.

Fear is a funny thing. I realize that it exists as a survival mechanism, but at the same time, it often robs us, cripples us, and stops us dead in our tracks. While I continued to grow up and make progress in my life past March 3, 1991, the fear that grabbed me that day never quite let me go.

Though I had suppressed what I had seen, more than twenty years later, the raw emotion and fear I had internalized from the Rodney King beating could still fight their way back to the surface whenever I was in a tense or uneasy situation or environment. I unconsciously carried that beating, King's arrest, and the following events that led to the LA Riots of 1992 with me wherever I went. I can see now how they have shaped my decisions and erected barriers in certain areas of my life over the years.

Fear was alive and well in my mind, and as real as it had been the day it had been born.

MARRIAGE FEARS

The more I thought about it, the more I didn't want to get married.

Okay, maybe somewhere deep down I *did* want to get married—I mean, I love my wife, my children, and the life we share today—but at a young age, I wasn't thinking about marriage because I *wanted* it. At that age, it was kind of scary to me. I was only thinking about it because I had hit *that point* in my life.

Just like at one point in my life buying comic books had been the thing to do, going to the arcade was the thing to do, attending junior high school dances was the thing to do, going to parties after high school football games was the thing to do … I was in the season of life where everyone around me was starting to talk about marriage. I was in my mid-to-late twenties and marriage was the next natural stage for the relationships many of us were in, so … might as well go for it, right?

But the fear was real. And it wasn't just your typical commitment jitters. Deep down, I knew that I would not make a great husband. I was egotistical, selfish, stubborn, and lacking in empathy. (There—I said it!) And even though I didn't know quite how to voice it at the time, I was terrified that my love and sacrifice *would not be reciprocated*. That I would not get back out of the relationship what I put in. That I would give so much of myself that there would be nothing left for me. That I would go out onto a ledge … and remain there alone. Or worse, be left to plummet to my death.

So, I never fully committed to any relationship. I never gave 100 percent of myself. It was all about economics and risk management … or so I told myself at the time. A safety measure. I didn't pay for dinner unless I knew that my date would pay for the next one. I never gave a massage unless I knew for a *fact* I would receive one in return. If I were to give all of my love to someone without a guarantee that I would get all of *their* love in return … it wasn't a deal I was willing to make.

There are, of course, no guarantees in love, and my fearful outlook was ultimately very damaging. My fear had ruined countless relationships and even some friendships over the years, and yet I couldn't let it go. It was keeping me safe, I told myself. The fear was a survival tactic. No one was going to *use* me.

No one was going to make promises to me that they couldn't keep. No one was going to get my hopes up, only to leave me standing there alone, kicking the curb, waiting for them to show up. The potential pain was simply not worth the risk.

Eventually, though, because I was at *that point* in my life, marriage became a thing that I went along with, just like the junior high dances and the high school football game parties. I gave in and got married. But I never fully committed myself to the marriage, and, perhaps predictably, the marriage sucked.

I couldn't—or, more egregiously, *wouldn't*—let go of the fear that bound me up and fenced me in. I couldn't give 100 percent of myself away because the fear told me it wasn't safe to do so. And I trusted the fear. The fear was known. The fear was comfortable. I had dug my claws into the fear, and I was *not* letting go.

I remember a mentor telling me, "Jamil, the walls we build up to keep out sadness and hurt are also the ones that keep out the joy." But I didn't care. Certain security was worth the price of uncertain joy.

It's like when you're a little kid, and you have to make the decision between getting out of bed in the middle of the night to use the bathroom, thus risking being killed and eaten by monsters, or you could stay safe in your bed and risk peeing yourself. For me, the fear was so true and so real that often I simply wet the bed.

They said, "She is NOT the problem; you are. You can just as easily create a story that serves you and your marriage instead of the story you've made up that doesn't serve you."

— THINK LIFE *is* DIFFERENT

As an adult, if I gave myself away unconditionally to my wife, if I loved her, if I trusted her, if I had faith, if I honored her and the process ... I would be giving in. I would be risking everything and potentially gaining nothing.

Fear sure is interesting, isn't it?

FAITH AND FEAR

I grew up in a church that seemed to have services that never ended. Not only did they never end, but it felt like there was some kind of service or other happening every day. And in my family, if there was a service going on, you had to be there. No excuses.

There were a lot of rules in church. You had to sit up straight. You had to face front. You could say this but not that. You could do this but not that. You could stand there or sit there but not *there*. If you were a girl, you couldn't wear your dress above your knee. And with every rule violation, there was always the chance you might get a one-way ticket to hell.

I heard a lot of things like, "Ooooh, child! Did she really come to church in that skimpy dress that's above her knees? She's got herself a one-way ticket to hell."

And: "Oh, my gooooodness! Did you hear about Deacon John? About what he did and about that girl he was with? He'd better repent and start speaking in tongues, or he's got himself a one-way ticket to hell."

And: "Did you see Sister Kelly? You didn't see that new car she bought? She got that new BMW 7 Series, knowing good and damn well she ain't contributing to the building fund. She don't have no problem flaunting that luxury car, though! Having all of that money? It's a one-way ticket to hell."

Because of my upbringing, I thought about flames, death, destruction, fire, hell, and the rapture *all the time*. I had learned that, when the day came, all of the good kids around me would fly up into heaven to enjoy everlasting life. But the bad kids—kids like me—who cussed a little bit, or who made fun of Bishop Desmond after he fell asleep in the corner during the service, or who giggled at Sister Jackie when she sprang up and spoke in tongues during the same song every Sunday morning during offering ...

Well. We had a one-way ticket to hell.

No matter what I was or wasn't, no matter what I did or didn't do, I was still getting that ticket. Impure thoughts? Hell. Disobeyed my mom? Hell. Gluttony? Hell. Missed a Sunday service? You got it—hell. The question wasn't whether or not I was going. The question was *when*.

So, every day, I walked around, waiting for the fiery gates to open up and devour me. I was literally afraid to do or say anything that might tip the scales. I didn't speak my mind. I snuck food to eat in secret. I was terrified to talk to girls. I didn't want to screw up. I couldn't risk messing up or having Satan misinterpret my actions. The fiery furnaces of hell were waiting for me.

Needless to say, as I got older, I developed a really strange relationship with faith, religion, and God. The fear of an eternity in hell was still deeply real for me, still echoing in every action I took and every word I said. I realized that living with this massive level of fear was unhealthy and decided that it would be a good idea to escape it.

So ... what did I do? What any logical young man would do, of course. I got a huge tattoo that covered my entire chest. In my defense, it was my first tattoo, and I figured I'd better go big or go home. The tattoo consisted of two crosses—one on each pectoral muscle—and in between read the word *Unashamed*.

Most people who see this tattoo automatically jump to the wrong conclusion: that I'm just very loudly unapologetic about whatever it may appear my religion or faith might be. However, I actually got the tattoo as an act of defiance against the fear the church had instilled in me for so many years.

It was basically my way of throwing down the gauntlet, a challenge to the mental fatigue I experienced from feeling like every single thing I did was wrong in the sight of the church. It was me saying, "I'm unashamed to be me ... and whatever happens, happens." It was me tearing up my one-way ticket to hell.

But even this bold move did not dispel the fear. It would take years and *lots* of work on myself for that to happen.

F.E.A.R.: FALSE EVIDENCE APPEARING REAL

Every shred of fear my mind and body had ever contained decided to manifest the day I launched my business. It was as though every one of those fears I'd thought were long gone had lingered, held a conference, and made a unanimous decision to invade my life again. All at once.

Every instance of limited confidence, low self-esteem, procrastination, hiding in the face of danger or discomfort, and constant not-enough-ness descended. I became terrified to perform even the simplest tasks. They weren't hard—they were tasks a five-year-old could easily do—but my fears of "How will I look?" and "What will they say?" paralyzed me and kept me in a cycle of inactivity.

I knew I had to drive clients to my business and market what I was doing, but the fear kept me thinking, "What if they think I'm trying to sell them?"

I knew our programs could bring hope to people's lives, but all I could focus on was, "What will they think of me?"

I knew I was called to serve in a marketplace ministry, but "What if I'm not good enough?" and "What if they find out I don't really know what I'm doing?" plagued me day and night.

I knew I wanted to create a better and brighter future for my son, but "What if they think I'm just trying to get money from them?" and "Will they think I'm a fraud?" kept me from living out that truth.

Fear grabbed hold of me just like it had after the Rodney King beating, just like it did when I couldn't release my ego in my marriage, and just like it had back when I knew for a fact that the jaws of hell were waiting to open for me. It was so fundamentally *real* and so *true* for me that there was nothing I could do about it.

Until there was.

They shouted,
"EVERYTHING
YOU WANT IS
ON THE OTHER
SIDE OF FEAR."

— THINK LIFE *is* DIFFERENT

GOD SPEAKS AT WALMART

It was a crisp night in December, and the weather was right on the verge of comfortably chilly and oh-my-goodness-I'm-freezing. My wife and I had set out north along the California coast toward our favorite vacation spot, and I was looking forward not only to spending time with her but also to reflecting on myself, my fears, and my limiting beliefs.

Because at that time, everything in my life was *just south of okay*. My marriage, my finances, my business, my role and behavior as a husband/father, my life … it was all just a notch below okay.

I had figured some things out in my business and knew how we would need to position our offering and program to attract clients. My individual client base was at an all-time high, but I didn't know how to expand the organization to bring in more business partners. It was too scary for me to even contemplate.

In short, I was ready for a breakthrough, and I hoped this trip would deliver.

We traveled for hours and exhausted all of our normal road trip pastimes (slug bug, CD sing-alongs, car salsa dancing), and eventually decided to pick up food and water for our hotel room to cut down on the cost of eating at restaurants for every meal.

Blinker on, we made a quick right exit and there it was: a Walmart. And not just any Walmart—a *Super* Walmart. We parked, and, excited to stretch our cramped legs, which felt as if rigor mortis had set in, we headed inside. "Amanda, grab some cheese, yogurt, egg whites, and red wine … I'll get the toiletries!" I called and beelined toward the appropriate aisles.

That's when it happened. About twenty feet in front of me was an elderly woman, maybe in her mid-sixties. She was accompanied by two boys who couldn't have been older than eleven or twelve, whom I assumed must have been her grandchildren, though I could have been wrong. She sat heavily in one of those motorized scooters you see people riding at amusement parks, and through the gray hair hanging over her face, I could see she was out of breath.

Every once in a while, she needed the assistance of the two boys to get in and out of her scooter, and when I saw how much weight she was carrying and how mightily she was gasping for air, my heart broke for her. When I saw the grace, love, and humility the boys showed in helping her, my heart broke again, and I remembered with renewed clarity exactly who I wanted to be.

My profession, my business, and my purpose was to help others. That was it. It wasn't about me or my ego or my fears or my questions or my hang-ups. It was about helping other people live healthy, happy, and fulfilling lives.

And it was nothing I hadn't done before. I had already coached over one hundred clients through their own weight-loss journeys. I had heard their struggles, borne witness to their silent cries, and seen miracles take place as they worked toward their own personal victories.

So, when I saw this woman, I knew I could help her. I held the key that would unlock so much suffering inside her and set her free from so many of her pains and troubles. I wanted to approach her, even if just to say, "Hi."

But I didn't.

It was almost as if I had a tiny person perched on each of my shoulders, arguing with each other about what I should or shouldn't do. The figure on my right shoulder said, "There are no coincidences! What if last night this woman prayed for someone like you to come into her life? What if you have been uniquely placed in her path to help her?"

But the figure on my left shoulder countered, "If you say anything, she's going to think you're a weirdo and that you're judging her for being fat. She has her grandbabies with her, and they'll probably be embarrassed too. You're a young Black man, and if you walk up to her, she'll be startled at best and terrified at worst."

For a good five minutes, these two little shoulder-figures snipped back and forth at each other, weighing my dilemma. And while they argued, I followed the woman and did not let her out of my sight, trying to pretend I was looking for some long-lost grocery item.

Finally, one of the little shoulder-people won out—and I left the Walmart.

Head hung low, I followed Amanda to the car and plopped into the passenger seat beside her, completely lost in thought. As I stared into the depths of my own personal abyss, Amanda gently asked in a way only she could, "What's wrong?"

I told her everything that had just taken place, including my suspicion that God had literally placed that woman in my path for me to help. I felt like my encounter with her had been my chance to make a difference, and I had let it pass me by.

"Well, if that's the way you feel," Amanda exclaimed, "then go back in there and talk to her! You're amazing! You've got this."

With my spirit renewed and a newfound connection with my mission, I ran back inside the Walmart. I was like a heat-seeking missile searching for my target, no longer just focused on walking up and down the aisles but performing an intentional dance in seeking out this woman whose life I was going to change.

Aisle after aisle, and no sight of the woman. No gray hair, no electric scooter, no kind young boys helping their grandma. I took another dance around the store, and she still wasn't there. I waited outside of the women's restroom in vain. I took a third lap around the Walmart with no sign of her ... and realized that I had probably missed my chance.

I blinked as the realization fully sank in, bruising my confidence and battering my ego on the way down. I walked back to the car, feeling more disappointed than I had in years, and sank back into my seat beside Amanda, eyes unfocused, heart racing.

I knew she was talking to me, but I couldn't really hear what she was saying. All I could hear was a gigantic rushing sound in my ears, signaling the tsunami of emotion that was rising, impossible to stop. I began to weep then, harder than I had ever wept in my life.

I think Amanda thought I was crying because I couldn't find the woman, but in all actuality, that was only a small part of it. At the heart of it, I was breaking down because I was tired of letting fear run my life. I was torn and exhausted and devastated, and, once and for all, I was *done*.

From March 3, 1991 until that moment in Walmart, fear had dominated my life. And I was done with it. I was done being afraid. I was done letting fear rule me. I was embarrassed and tired, and I just didn't want to play that game anymore. From there on out, I forged an agreement with myself—I was in control. Not fear.

There's a poem that has sat in my heart for many years now, one of those poems that, when you read it, you feel like it's describing your entire life. It's called "Autobiography in Five Short Chapters," by Portia Nelson. Coincidentally, I stumbled upon it that evening as I reflected on what had happened at the Walmart:

Chapter One

I walk down the street.
There is a deep hole in the sidewalk.
I fall in.
I am lost ... I am helpless.
It isn't my fault.
It takes forever to find a way out.

Chapter Two

I walk down the same street.
There is a deep hole in the sidewalk.
I pretend I don't see it.
I fall in again.
I can't believe I am in this same place.
But, it isn't my fault.
It still takes me a long time to get out.

Chapter Three

I walk down the same street.
There is a deep hole in the sidewalk.
I *see* it is there.
I still fall in ... it's a habit ... but,
my eyes are open.
I know where I am.
It is *my* fault. I get out immediately.

They said, "Most people are experts in ruining momentum. Don't be that person."

— THINK LIFE *is* DIFFERENT

Chapter Four
I walk down the same street.
There is a deep hole in the sidewalk.
I walk around it.

Chapter Five

I walk down another street.

For years, I'd been walking down the same street, stepping in the same deep holes of fear, and wondering why I wasn't finding success. Not until that day did it occur to me to simply walk down another street.

THE RICHEST PLACE ON EARTH

It's been said that the richest place on Earth isn't the oil-rich soil of Saudi Arabia or the high-tech mecca of Silicon Valley. Rather, it's the graveyard—because there, you will find all of the books that were never written, the songs that were never sung, the inventions that were never shared, the cures that were never discovered, and all of the other hopes and dreams of humankind that were never fulfilled.

Our most powerful possessions are buried in the ground with us because we cannot let go of our fears. We are all too often too afraid to take the necessary steps, stick with difficult problems, work through discomforts, and experience real breakthroughs. But you have a superpower that you can tap into, if you allow yourself to tap into it.

Let fear be your rocket fuel.

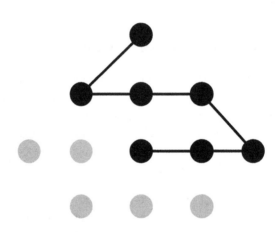

Shift Seven

It's Bigger Than Me

"The breezes at dawn have secrets to tell you …"

– RUMI

Could it be possible that your life is *not actually your life?*

Could it be possible that there are forces outside of yourself, directing and hinting at what must be done for a larger purpose you were meant to fulfill?

Remember the words of the poet Rumi that we discussed back in Shift Five?

The breezes at dawn have secrets to tell you.

Don't go back to sleep.

You must ask for what you really want.

Don't go back to sleep.

What if you tucked in your ego for the night, got all quiet and still, and listened to those whispers that linger at the edge of your imagination? What would you hear? What would those breezes at dawn have to tell you?

What if we called a timeout on working and hustling and *doing*, just for a little while, and focused on being *done?*

THE NEED TO *DO*

Early on in my coaching business, I was a doer. A hustler. A fighter. I worked harder and pushed myself further than ever before. I was never fully satisfied in my quest for success, and I hunted down opportunities like a starving man hunts for food. Success was waiting for me at the end of the road, and I was an unstoppable force heading straight toward it. Success was the target, and I was the arrow.

My desire for success wasn't just a *want*—it was a *need*. A drive. I needed to show all the naysayers, the people who laughed at me and didn't share my vision, that I could *do* it. I needed to prove to them that I was worth something, that I could be somebody. That I could make success *happen.* That I could fight my way toward it.

Hell, I had to prove it to *myself.* Every day, I would look for people to impact and breakthroughs to have. I was determined to find success.

I asked, "Teacher, why do they do that?" He said, "Rarely do we find men who willingly engage in hard, solid thinking. There is an almost universal quest for easy answers and half-baked solutions. Nothing pains some people more than having to think."

— THINK LIFE *is* DIFFERENT

I was determined to make it happen. My whole life was all about making things happen. In sports, relationships, school, and at work—*I made things happen.*

But for every two steps forward I would take, life seemed determined to set me two steps back. No matter how hard I pushed, how hard I fought, life pushed back with an equal and opposite force. The success I was chasing seemed as elusive as a wisp of cloud.

Around this time, my desperate search for success took me down the rabbit hole of personal development, and I began to read books by Dr. Wayne Dyer, Eckhart Tolle, Gary Zukav, and more. I dove into Zukav's *The Seat of the Soul* and read something truly revolutionary to my mindset.

What would happen if I simply stopped fighting so hard? What would happen if I slowed down? What would happen if I stopped *doing* ... and simply allowed myself to *be done to*? What if I simply ... *accepted?*

The concept was entirely alien to me and definitely not something people who were already self-actualized like I was did, but hey ... I was so desperate for success I was willing to try anything.

THE SAN MATEO STORY

Just two months after I left my full-time job to build my health coaching business, I got a text message late one night from my friend Stacy. She was inviting me to travel up to northern California to celebrate her birthday.

My plane ticket would cost a couple hundred dollars, which was challenging for me at the time, and the party was only a few days away, but I *immediately* felt a strong urge, almost like a gravitational pull, to attend. Against all reason, I felt like I *needed* to be there.

I leaned over to Amanda, who was still half-asleep, and whispered, "Stacy just invited me up north to her birthday party, and I *really* feel like I am supposed to be there." She agreed, probably to get rid of me for a couple days, and I left for San Mateo that Thursday evening.

In the two-and-a-half days I spent in northern California with Stacy, miracle after miracle happened in an insane sequence that I have since dubbed "The San Mateo Story." Here's what happened:

During my flight north, I thought about sharing my health coaching program with Stacy. I decided to share my own personal weight loss story with her and figured I would share all of my amazing client testimonials with her as well. Maybe she would go for it, or maybe I would simply get to spend some quality time with my friend. Either way, it was a win.

Unbeknownst to me, Stacy had really been struggling with her health, self-confidence, and weight, and the very second I mentioned the health coaching program, she jumped. She was so excited to have finally found something that would work for her.

Now, Stacy's sister, Kim, lived directly downstairs from her and had also been trying to reach her own health goals using a series of at-home workout videos. Stacy didn't think that the videos were doing her any good and insisted that she and I pay Kim a visit.

During our visit, Kim was raving about her workout videos, so much so that I decided not to share my health program pitch with her. After several hours, I felt the exhaustion sink in and excused myself to go back to Stacy's apartment to rest, but Stacy stopped me.

"We didn't stay here this long for you to *not* share your health program with my sister," she said. So, I explained to Kim what the program entailed, and Stacy eagerly piped up that she was committed to doing it. And with that, the workout videos were out, and Kim was in.

As we stood there in Kim's living room, I felt a tinge of intuition and decided to pay attention to it. I mentioned how excited I was for the both of them to start feeling better and to start losing weight, but I had to be honest—I felt like someone close to them was in need of our health program even more than they were.

Simultaneously, they turned to each other and said, "Brenda."

"Who's Brenda?" I asked.

It turns out Brenda was their cousin, a woman with several severe medical conditions who had suffered from health problems her entire life.

Kim told me that she was going to call Brenda first thing on Monday morning, and with that, we all retired to bed.

The next morning, Stacy received a call from Kim, who was ecstatic. "You won't believe this," Kim said, "but I just got off the phone with Brenda to tell her about this health program we're going to start. She was literally in line at Costco to buy a different program and said that if I would have called her even five minutes later, it would have been too late!"

The chain reaction kept happening, and more and more people in Stacy's life realized they needed my health coaching services. Next up were Toni and Matt, and then Bonnie and Dave, and then Kari, Ozzi, Zeke, and more for a total of *thirty-two individuals*.

Within the span of my two-and-a-half-day trip, *thirty-two people* had dedicated their lives to changing.

Over the next several months, stories of success poured in. Phone calls, thank you notes, and tears of gratitude and joy rained down from all of the people whose lives were shifting and changing for the better. It was incredible to witness, and that was when I began to realize … *this is bigger than me*.

This wasn't me hustling and working hard and fighting and pushing and *doing*. This was me being centered, laying down my ego, following my instincts, listening to those guiding whispers, and allowing myself to be *done unto*.

Did I do the work? Yes. Did I talk to people? Yes. Did I share my story and vision? Yes. But all the while, the whispers were there—the gravitational pull remained strong. I just needed to give in to it, follow its call, and stay within the flow. This was a *shift* of monumental proportions.

FORGETTING OUR PURPOSE

Purpose is one of those funny little words that gets tossed around without really ever being questioned or investigated too closely. Everyone seems to be searching for it, but very few people seem to know what it means to find it.

When I ask people, "Why are you here?" the overwhelming response is, "I don't know." So, I rephrase the question: "Okay ... why were you born?" And again, the response is usually, "I don't know."

Try it for yourself—write down the names of ten people in your family, place of work, social circle, school, etc., and ask them, "Why were you born?" Nine out of ten will likely respond, "I don't know."

Now, a few years ago, I would have had the same response. In fact, I *did* have the same response. Thinking about why I existed or for what greater purpose I had been born was *hard*, and life was so distracting. There was too much work, too much stress, too many arguments, too much traffic, too much Facebook and Instagram, too much with kids and life and everything going on all at once.

And yet ... I wondered. In between the moments of busyness and distraction I would get a sensation of goosebumps, the hint of a whisper, the fleeting sense that I was here, living, breathing, and existing, for a larger purpose—but what that purpose *was*, I didn't know.

Yet I felt that at some point in time, I *had known* the answer to that question. I just hadn't lived the answer in a long time, and it had slipped into some distant memory. It's incredibly easy for us to forget our purpose. But thankfully, there is a way to discover it again.

As the father of three small children, I have noticed that purpose reveals itself early on in our lives. All three of my kids live, eat, and sleep under the same roof, alongside the same parents, sharing the same experiences in the same environment. And yet all three are so completely different from each other, and in their differences, each begins to reveal their unique purpose.

The ways in which they behave, the manner in which they treat others, the subtle (and not-so-subtle) ways they gravitate toward the arts, toward sports, toward learning, toward empathetic leadership—these are all glimmers of the people they were made to be. Glimpses of their purposes being revealed.

Unfortunately, this purpose is destined to be forgotten, until they remember it again as adults. Allow me to explain.

They said, "People don't care how much you know, young man, until they know how much you care."

— THINK LIFE *is* DIFFERENT

From the time I was a little boy, I had a unique ability to bring people together—an innate passion for connecting people. In grade school, I would encourage one group of friends to play with another group of friends, and I would help resolve my friends' arguments and issues. I always fought for the underdog and stood up to authority on behalf of my peers if I felt like some sort of injustice had occurred (which got me into trouble more often than not).

As I got older, people continued coming to me with their problems, finding me trustworthy and capable of listening to and helping them. I would even find myself communing with and trying to help strangers. One of my most often-used phrases was, "I just met you, and I have no idea why I'm telling you this, but ..."

For whatever reason, I never thought much of what I was doing until I re-examined it years later as an adult, in an intentional search for my purpose. I realized that it's so easy for us to forget those initial childhood whispers of purpose and to get caught up in what everyone else is doing and what we feel like we're "supposed" to do.

We try so hard to be like everyone else that we forget how to be ourselves.

I had to very intentionally rediscover my gifts and purpose in adulthood, and in order to fully live into it, I had to understand it and claim it as my own.

CREATE IN ME A CLEAN HEART

In the summer of 1999, I went on one of my first big mission trips. I was fresh out of high school and full of big ideas, wanting desperately to make a difference in the world. So, I leapt at the opportunity to travel to Armenia and impact the lives of others in my own way.

I got a job selling Cutco cutlery to fund my trip, and chances are, if you had a kitchen, living room, business, or church, I had probably contacted you about doing a product demonstration there. Within a few months, my trip was fully funded (and I was one of Cutco's top reps, but that's another story for another day), and I joyfully boarded my fifteen-hour flight to Yerevan.

My group and I traveled from city to city in Armenia, building houses, visiting the sick, feeding the hungry, helping the poor, praying with the youth, and playing soccer in Republic Square with the locals. It was unlike anything I had ever experienced before as an eighteen-year-old Black male—complicated and affirming and terrifying and powerful all at once.

I was in a city called Sevan when it happened.

We were helping the locals build a church, but the project was not going incredibly well. The city of Sevan was surrounded by water and the air and ground were heavy with moisture. The plans we were working from needed significant modification, and we spent more time standing around figuring things out than acting and executing. The day was extremely hot, and after several hours of start-and-stop work, one of the youth pastors ushered us inside of a stone building to escape the heat.

As we waited within this stone structure, someone began to sing a hymn, and we all joined in:

> Create in me a clean heart, O God,
> And renew a right spirit within me.
> Create in me a clean heart, O God,
> And renew a right spirit within me.
> Cast me not away from Thy presence;
> Take not Thy holy Spirit from me.
> Restore unto me the joy of Thy salvation;
> And renew a right spirit within me.

We sang this song over and over again, twenty times or more, but it was what happened *during* the song that stood out.

My eyes were closed, but out of nowhere a flash of light hit me, and an image appeared within it. A voice spoke: "You are a prophet. You will restore the lives and hearts of many."

I was so terrified that my eyes flew open, and I looked around the room, wondering if anyone else had seen what I had. It was the most deeply *real* experience I had ever had, but it was also the most frightening.

See, I didn't believe in any of that hocus-pocus stuff. I grew up exposed to people running up and down the church aisles, speaking in tongues, and falling on the floor in between the pews, but I had never really believed in any of it.

Let's face it: I was a cool eighteen-year-old kid from California. Visions and that kind of stuff didn't *happen* to people like me. And they certainly weren't things we talked about in my inner circle.

So, just as quickly as it had happened, I dismissed it.

PURPOSE REVEALED BUT NOT UNDERSTOOD

If you read enough comic books and watch enough movies, you know that even superheroes forget who they are sometimes. Captain America faces doubt. Superman feels despair. Iron Man sinks into alcoholism. And every once in a while, even Wonder Woman needs to be reminded of what she stands for.

For many of us, this purpose-related amnesia becomes permanent.

Have you ever felt like there was a tremendous calling for your life … but you weren't quite sure what it was? Have you ever felt an odd familiarity pulling you toward something … but you just couldn't put your finger on it? Have you ever felt frustrated because you couldn't pinpoint quite what you wanted for your life?

Have you ever felt in your heart that there was something bigger out there, waiting for you? Have circumstances ever convened to hammer you over the head with information you simply refused to understand?

All of this has happened to me, and I'll bet the same is true for you.

One night in Cusco, Peru, I found myself in a mountaintop hut 11,200 feet above sea level. My friends and I were waiting for a shaman to guide us through our first (and potentially only) *Ayahuasca* experience. After a grueling and intense six hours (which I'll fully discuss in an upcoming book), many truths were revealed to me. Most important were the words I heard, which I believe to be from God Himself: *You are My greatest creation, and you are here to do My work.* Throughout the entire trip, one word kept surfacing and echoing through my mind and spirit: *Prophet. Prophet. Prophet.*

They reminded me,
"For true happiness,
relinquish your ego."

— THINK LIFE *is* DIFFERENT

One year later, I was in a one-on-one session with my personal development coach, Dave, when he asked me that all-important question: "Jamil, who are you?"

Here's the funny thing—even though I knew the answer, the words that automatically fell out of my mouth were, "I don't know."

I hadn't second-guessed myself or even doubted the truth of the answer I had been about to give. But I said "I don't know" at the last second because I was more concerned with what Dave would think than I was with speaking my own truth. I had gotten in my own way.

Thankfully, Dave asked me a second time: "Jamil, *who are you?*"

And I told the truth this time: "I am God's greatest creation, here to do His work."

Dave nodded, satisfied, and said, "You know what that sounds like to me? *A prophet.*"

FOLLOW YOUR INTUITION, FOLLOW THE VOICE

My mother stayed with us recently, and while I was driving her from my home back to the airport, she said something to me that, at this point, was not incredibly surprising. Want to know what she said?

She said, "Jamil, I always knew you were a prophet."

Normally, these words would have freaked me out, but not this time. This time, they were expected, and this time, they rang true.

All in all, it's pretty simple—if you have a life, you have a purpose, and you can tap into that purpose whenever you're ready. Every single one of the 7.8 billion people on this planet has a reason for being here, and if you find that you are suffering in any way, I would posit that you are not following your true calling or purpose.

When I was chasing someone else's dreams and not my own, I was miserable. But when I quieted my inner monologue, sat still, and listened, I began to understand not only what my own purpose was but what I should do to fulfill it.

Life is bigger than you. But at the same time, you are bigger than life.

Now is the time to put yourself back into alignment with your true self and ask: "Why am I here?" and "What is my purpose?" Being able to answer these questions is the next shift, the next superpower that you can and will unlock.

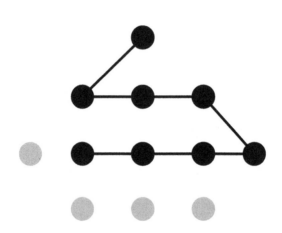

Shift Eight

Tell Your Story

*"There is no greater agony than bearing
an untold story inside you."*

– MAYA ANGELOU

Microsoft has a story. IBM has a story. Apple has a story. Disney has a story. The United States of America has a story. California has a story. Every tree planted in the ground has a story. Every soul has a story. You have a story. I have a story.

The problem was that for most of my life, I recognized that things were happening to me, and that I was progressing through life in a linear fashion, but I never really thought about it as a cohesive *story*. I didn't think that the things I did and said really *meant* anything when taken as a whole. I didn't know that I had the power to affect tens, hundreds, thousands, and even millions of other people around me.

In short, I did not fully understand *The Story of Jamil*, and I did not know what it meant or how it could impact others.

To be fair, I wasn't a big company like Microsoft, IBM, Apple, or Disney, with a mission statement set on changing the world. I didn't have a giant platform, political or otherwise, from which to share my story. I wasn't even especially remarkable as an individual, like Maya Angelou or Oprah, so how important could my story even *be*?

However, since then, I have learned many truths that I'd like to share with you in this shift. Namely:

1. *You have a story.*

2. *Your story is important.*

3. *You impact others' lives when you share your story. However, you also impact lives negatively by not sharing it.*

4. *If you tell your story with the boldness and passion of a large company such as Disney or Apple, you can impact lives on a scale that staggers the imagination.*

Yes! You have a story. I have a story. And those stories are more important than you ever thought.

Because on the other side of your true, authentic story lies *freedom*.

They whispered, "Is that thought serving you?"

— THINK LIFE *is* DIFFERENT

WHAT WOULD JAMIL HAVE WANTED
TO KNOW SEVEN YEARS AGO?

Seven years ago, I played things very close to the chest. I was the master of masking issues, and I only allowed people to see a very carefully curated facade. No visible problems. No visible worries. I was doing great.

I had a nice pharmaceutical sales job with Johnson & Johnson. I had a company car, an expense account, a smart and beautiful wife, a beautiful son with perfect hair and a perfect skin tone ... everything was great.

Except ... nothing was great. The facade was a lie.

The *truth* was that I was stuck in year two of a very intense depression. I was frustrated relationally, spiritually, sexually, financially, physically, and emotionally. At points, I thought about taking my own life.

And while I worked incredibly hard, and I knew that no one was coming to save me, I still carried this sense of *waiting*—waiting for my wife to change so I could be happy, waiting for the next onslaught of bosses to be hired so I could be successful, waiting for my life to turn around, for that dream house to open up, for me to feel like less of a failure.

I constantly looked to others to set the standards, and all I saw were their happy faces. They were doing great—at least, from the outside. They were successful, with new houses, happy marriages, and family members who could assist them financially.

Stuck in my 700-square-foot condo, with a stagnant job, a wife who didn't want to change, a God who had forgotten about me, and not *nearly* enough money, I felt like I was sinking into quicksand. I felt that every forward step someone else took sent me two steps back. I felt like all of my hard work was for nothing, and that all of my money was being squandered.

I felt like I could not keep the promises I had made to myself as a little boy, sitting in a makeshift room in a rundown house, on a rundown lot, in an affluent city.

As we've talked about in a previous shift, despite my mindset, my business was still fairly successful. In 2013, I was invited to speak at an upper-level seminar, despite the fact that I still didn't think I knew what I was doing.

They were going to give me about ten minutes to speak about my journey and how I had achieved such success in just ten short months. I was nervous—really, *really* nervous—because I was going to be telling this story in front of more than two thousand people. I still felt like a fraud, or like I hadn't really been successful at all. And it was my first time on the main stage.

I didn't necessarily prepare for the talk because right before it I had a falling out with some business partners and mentors. So, I went out onto the stage and stared at the audience, a crowd of more than two thousand people waiting to hear my "incredible" story. What wisdom would I share? What wisdom did I *have*?

My talk ended up being about two minutes. Essentially, I went up to the edge of the stage and said, "This is no big deal. I just went out and talked to some people. And I walked the beach."

That was my pathetic talk.

When I left the stage, an ex-president of a New York Stock Exchange company came up to me. He was probably one of the most handsome African American men I've ever seen—debonair, polished, aged mid-sixties with the spirit of a thirty-year-old. He pulled me to the side and said, "I've seen a lot of talented young entrepreneurs come through here, but this is my first time seeing you. Where did you come from?"

I told him, jokingly, "You know, I just talked to some people about that …"

But he shook his head at me and said, "No, young man. What you just shared on the stage didn't help anyone. I've seen a lot of people try to be successful with a lot longer of a timeframe." He paused. "What's your *true, authentic story?*"

And for the first time in my entire life, I shared it.

I poured everything out to this man who looked like Billy Dee Williams. I told him where I came from, where I had gone, and where

I had been just a year before. I told him why I was so driven, passionate, and invested in what I wanted to do with my business. I told him how I wanted to help myself and other people.

I started talking about my son and how, just ten months prior, Amanda and I had been talking about getting separate apartments. I told him about how divorce papers had come around three times, and how I downright refused to have another man raise my son.

I told him that every day when I woke up, I was chasing freedom.

That beautiful man nodded and said, "That's the story that's going to change lives and resurrect cities. That will bring nations together. *That's* the story the people needed to hear today—not the other one! It served no one, not humanity, and not even *you!*"

And at that moment, I had another shift. I realized that my story wasn't just *my story*. It was something that I owed others—the experiences I'd had, the life I had lived. It was all important because it could help other people to learn, grow, find success, and continue in their own stories.

Stories were full of value. And *denying* my true, authentic story to those two-thousand-plus people gathered in the audience for this conference meant that *I had denied them that value*. Some had even been looking specifically for a breakthrough, and I could have provided it. I could have changed lives and businesses with a short ten-minute story.

Once again, my ego had gotten in the way. But I knew now, and would know every day going forward, that telling my true, authentic story would be a vehicle of value, meaning, and freedom for thousands.

THE ABORTION THREAD

I remember the first time I took a risk on social media, and I talked about the time I asked my wife to have an abortion of our first son. I was incredibly nervous and scared because of the negative backlash I thought I would receive.

But instead, the exact opposite happened. A long and thoughtful conversation was sparked. People I didn't even know messaged me day and night. That one message turned into a series about men who had asked their wives for an abortion.

I realized that this was an issue people *needed* to talk about and that there was a dearth of discussion about abortion in the public space. The thing I had been so afraid to talk about was the one thing men and women *needed* to talk about because everyone was so damn scared.

I expanded the series and opened up with more stories about how I had been emotionally abusive to my wife, because hurt people hurt people. People flooded my inbox, asking me how I got over it, moved past it, healed my marriage, and grew.

Most people use social media as an ESPN highlight reel, carefully framing the best parts of their lives to put on display. But the highlight reel doesn't give the whole story. It's not there to serve others—it's just there to serve our own egos.

Every game has a highlight reel—whether the game is a win or loss, there are always some fantastic plays that can be showcased. But the highlight reel isn't what counts. What counts is whether or not you win the game.

I want my life to be a winning game, not just a highlight reel. And to win, we need to tell our true, authentic stories. It's the only way we can come together, grow, and learn.

Alwyn Cosgrove of Results Fitness tells a parable that hammers home this point wonderfully:

> A man fell into a hole and couldn't get out. A doctor walked by, and the man yelled up, "Can you help me? I can't get out!"
>
> The doctor wrote a prescription, threw it down into the hole, and walked away.
>
> A priest walked by, and the man yelled up, "Help! I've fallen into a hole and can't get out."
>
> The priest wrote a prayer on a piece of paper, threw it down to the man, and walked on.

Soon the man's friend walked by. "Hey, friend! I've fallen into this hole and can't get out. Can you help me?"

The friend said, "Sure," and jumped into the hole with his friend.

The man said, "Are you crazy? Now we're both stuck in this hole!"

But his friend said, "No, see, I've been in this hole before, and I know how to get out."

So, what's your story, *for real*? How can you win the game? And what can you share with others that will help them get out of the holes they're stuck in? Did you know your story IS your superpower if you'll allow it to be?

THE POWER OF TRUTH

My mother privately shared some incredibly painful stories with us growing up about the abuse she had received at her father's hands. He had raped and molested her as a child, and she had never spoken about it publicly.

When I was ten, my mother told me she was going to write a book about her father and expose the truth of his abusive ways. But for one reason or another, she never got around to it. Finally, a few years ago, she published her first book—*If Not Today, Maybe Tomorrow*—and in it, she told the whole truth about what her father had done. She named names and described horrible situations that no one should ever have to endure.

And with the publication of her book, several of my mother's cousins came forward and said that the same thing had happened to them too. They had just been too afraid to say anything until my mother had come forward and so bravely shared her truth.

Telling your story and hiding your story both have consequences, and they both have the power to ripple outward and affect, impact, and change people's lives. It's ultimately your choice regarding what you decide to share and what you decide to hold back.

But please remember, lies and misrepresentation don't help *anyone*. If you want to have a positive effect on the world, the marketplace, your ministry, and humanity, then I suggest you start telling your honest, authentic story.

HOW DO I UNDERSTAND AND TELL MY OWN STORY?

Let's go back to one of the principles we learned in Shift Seven: stop trying so hard to *do*, and simply let yourself be *done unto*.

Go to a quiet place, get comfortable, and take some deep breaths. If you're a person of faith, quiet your mind and ask God for direction. If you're not, try taking up meditation. It doesn't need to be spiritually guided—you just need to be in a place where your mind is open and receptive.

Let your mind drift as you think about your life and the things that make you the most uncomfortable. I can almost guarantee that's where to start. If it has been a struggle for you, it has likely been something many others are struggling with right now.

Finding your words to talk about these struggles will help others find theirs. This is how the ripple begins. Because when you equip others to share their truth, they will in turn do the same for those around them.

If you're having difficulty reflecting on your own life, that's okay. It might be a good idea to seek out a mentor or friend you trust who can hold the metaphorical mirror up to you. Ask them, "What do you think my story is?" and "What has value for others?" and "Where do you think would be a good place to start?"

You may also find yourself discrediting your own importance. It's hard for us to talk or think about ourselves sometimes, depending on how we were raised. This is another great time to turn to a friend you trust who will remind you of how amazing and important you are. I call these "reminding sessions." A reminding session can help you remember, "Damn, I'm kinda tight."

They said, "Don't start tomorrow until it is finished in your head."

— THINK LIFE *is* DIFFERENT

WHAT IF I DON'T HAVE A STORY?

I remember working with a coach who used to tell me, "I don't have a story like you. I've never had any of the struggles you talk about, and my life hasn't really been that interesting."

She truly wrestled with this because in her heart of hearts, she desperately wanted to touch others' lives and create that ripple effect. I told her that she was judging herself and needed to remove her ego from the equation. I told her that whether she believed she had a *good* story did not negate the fact that she still had a story to tell.

Your story—no matter how dull or boring it feels to you—can always help *someone*. There is always someone out there whose story will need the mirror of your own. Even if you don't feel like you've had terrible problems or overcome any significant struggles, *your voice still matters*. And depriving the world of your story is stealing value away from the people who need it to move forward.

Say your story is about all of the wealth and abundance you've been able to enjoy in your life, or all of the blessings God has bestowed upon you and your heritage. This is still an important story! Someone out there needs to hear it and can be positively changed by it. If it's your story, and if it's true, there is value in it.

Or maybe you can use your story to begin asking important questions. What motivates you about your story? What do you feel called to share? Why do you feel like the things that have happened in your life happened to *you*? What have you learned? How have you grown? Are you content? Resentful? Grateful? What are you expressing, and why?

No matter what it is, your story matters.

On the other side of your story is great value and freedom for others who need it. If you have an amazing gift, an amazing marriage, amazing children, an amazing ministry, then you still have a story. The fact that you're breathing right now lends credibility to that fact.

So, if you're looking to give back, I strongly suggest that you move forward and tell your story.

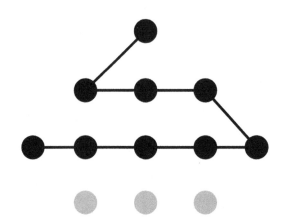

End Toxic Relationships

*"Stay away from negative people.
They have a problem for every solution."*

– ATTRIBUTED TO ALBERT EINSTEIN

One of the hardest things you will ever have to do in your life is break off a relationship.

Family units, inner circles, and tribes are integral to who we are as humans, and separating those tightly knit communities can be not only incredibly painful but downright unthinkable. It's unnatural and goes against our very instincts!

But … sometimes, it *needs* to be done.

I get a lot of pushback when I speak about this topic, and understandably so. Human relationships of all kinds are incredibly complex, and there are always extenuating circumstances and ways to justify a variety of behaviors. There's history and trust and understanding and love in the mix. There's also a sense of belonging that we feel like we must maintain at all costs.

There's even a sense of morality or honor involved—culturally, we tend to say things like "family first," "blood is thicker than water," and "best friends forever," and we make powerful vows of everlasting, eternal love at our wedding ceremonies.

Often, when I suggest in a coaching capacity that a relationship needs to be cut off or broken, the person I'm talking to will reject my suggestion, get defensive, or flat-out attack me.

And it makes sense! Of course we are going to reject advice that feels unnatural, just as our white blood cells attack unnatural, foreign objects within our bodies. Why would we willingly subject ourselves to something so painful?

I only advocate breaking off relationships that are harmful or toxic. But unfortunately, as much of history can attest, some of the best and most important things we can do for our lives come out of situations that are painful. Remember growth equals pain? In this case, pain can mean not only breaking off a relationship but breaking away from a community where we thought we were safe.

As human beings, one of our fundamental desires is for safety, comfort, security, and the knowledge that we are valued and loved.

We receive fulfillment of these desires within our families, tribes, and communities, which is why we cling to them so hard. It's why we're afraid to move across the country to a new city where we don't know anyone or why we're afraid to leave a group of coworkers for a new, better, higher-paying job.

But often, we need to painfully break ties and rearrange our social circles for our own greater good.

POISONOUS BELIEF SYSTEMS

There are a lot of people on this planet who mean well but still hurt people.

What would happen if you were drinking coffee with an enemy you hated, and they slipped some strychnine (a deadly poison) into your coffee, unnoticed?

You would drink the coffee and die.

Now, what would happen if you were drinking coffee with your mom, your best friend, your favorite cousin, and your pastor, and one of them accidentally knocked some strychnine into your coffee, unnoticed?

You would drink the coffee, and *you would still be just as dead.*

The people closest to you love you and have your best interests at heart—but from time to time, these loving, morally upright people may accidentally knock some strychnine into your coffee. Their intent is never to harm you, but through ignorance, clumsiness, or some sort of mental gymnastics, they did it anyway.

In real life, there isn't always strychnine lying around within easy contamination distance of your coffee. (I hope.) But there *are* things that are just as poisonous and even more prevalent—belief systems.

When I sit down with people and ask them what they want, they are often afraid to tell me the truth. They generally respond, "I don't know."

I nod and say, "Pretend you *did* know."

And they say, "Well, *realistically* …"

I tell them, "We're not talking *realistically*. We're talking about what you *want*."

They squirm a little and say, "Well, if it was *possible* …"

And again, I tell them, "No! What do you *actually want*?"

Finally, after doing this dance for a while, they say something like, "Well, Jamil, I've gotta tell you, I think I know what I want, but I'm a little nervous to say it."

I nod and give them space to speak. Usually, they continue with something like: "I really want to leave this full-time job …" or "I want a loving relationship …" or "I really want to have healthier finances …" or "I've never traveled anywhere …"

These are not weird, abnormal things to want. These are in fact very normal, very human things to want. And yet we find them *incredibly* hard to talk about. I've found that it's scary to tell people what you want because the minute you reveal what that is, they have the power to tear it down, destroy it, or dismiss it.

Now, the people you tell won't necessarily do this on purpose or at all. Perhaps you'll tell your husband or wife that you've always dreamed of traveling to Thailand or pursuing your MBA degree, and they'll be 100 percent on board. Perhaps they'll even want to go to Thailand with you or get an advanced degree of their own.

But sometimes, the people closest to us—yes, the people who *actively want the best for us*—let their own fears and issues tear down, destroy, or dismiss our wants. Let me explain.

Say there is a woman who wants to travel to Thailand, but when she expresses this desire to her husband, he yells, "What a stupid idea! What would you want to do that for?" Now, her husband doesn't necessarily want her to be unhappy. Chances are, he dislikes (or is afraid of) traveling or is worried for her safety. Maybe he's afraid that if she goes without him, she'll meet someone new or have a life-changing experience that he won't get to share.

They said, "Not everyone
will stay."

— THINK LIFE *is* DIFFERENT

Or say there's a little girl who wants to be a world-famous ballet dancer when she grows up. Her mother carefully warns her not to get her hopes up, not because she wants to crush her daughter's dreams, but because she's afraid those dreams are too big to come true. And dreams that don't come true are painful.

Maybe something like this has happened to you in your own life. The people who care about us are afraid we'll be hurt if what we want doesn't pan out, so they go ahead and destroy or deflate our dreams for us.

Or maybe they see our hopes and dreams and begin to feel afraid— afraid that if we change and accomplish our dreams, then they will be forced along with us into a change they're not comfortable with.

Or maybe they're afraid that we'll outpace or outgrow them.

Or maybe they're afraid that our passion project will pull them out of their comfort zone.

Or maybe they're afraid that our time in the limelight will shatter their ego (talking primarily to the men here with this one).

Or maybe they're afraid that our success means they will have to face their own failures.

Maybe they're asking, consciously or unconsciously, "If that works for you, what does it mean for *me*?"

LEAVING THE TRIBE COMES AT A COST

I grew up with a lot of dichotomies in my life. Half my siblings were Muslim, and half were Christian. Half my family were gang members for the Bloods, and half belonged to the Crips.

Now ask yourself: what would happen if a Crip suddenly had a new vision and decided to leave their gang? Well, they would get their ass beat. You do not get to leave an organization like that for free. Same with the Bloods.

Leaving a lifelong church or religious group can bring frighteningly similar consequences. Or imagine a lifelong Democrat who suddenly decides he's a conservative. Things aren't going to go incredibly well and might even get violent.

I see it in the coaching world, too, especially among religious people. Religious husbands may get threatened if the norms, roles, and customs of their wives change, so they try to pull them back in. It's less threatening if they know what "place" their wives are in.

I don't know if you've ever watched a bucket of crabs on the deck of a boat, but a similar phenomenon occurs: if one crab tries to escape the bucket, all of the other crabs will reach up to pull it back in.

Leaving the tribe comes at a cost.

We base our social lives on trends, norms, roles, and responsibilities. Tribes work best when everyone involved shares the same vision and follows the same rules. But once you see your own vision or begin to follow your own dreams, you may begin to affect others' comfortable roles and ruffle some feathers.

If you're reading this, chances are you're a person with vision. If and when you decide to meet your vision with action, other members in your tribe (or social circle, family, etc.) may begin to react in surprising and unexpected ways.

This may seem paranoid or cynical, but keep an eye on the people closest to you. They may love you and want what's best for you, but they also have their own needs, comfort, and survival to protect.

In the coaching world, we call this "WIIFM" thinking, as in, "What's in It For Me?"

For example, if a husband tells his wife that he's thinking of quitting his day job, following his passion, and making $20,000 per month doing health coaching, it may outwardly sound fantastic. But inwardly, the wife may suddenly be faced with a boatload of worries and fears about her own situation. She may think:

- *"Will I have to change my work situation to accommodate him?"*
- *"Will I need to start dieting and exercising?"*

- *"Am I going to have to do our kids' nighttime routines all alone now?"*
- *"Will this sudden, enormous shift in income make our marriage less equal?"*
- *"I really like our life the way it is now ... what if I don't want to change?"*
- *"What does all of this mean for* me*?"*

This can lead to knee-jerk or protective measures that dump the figurative strychnine into our figurative coffee.

I know this firsthand because the very same thing happened to me. The moment I decided to quit my full-time job, become a coach, and start a nontraditional business was the moment that some of the people closest to me started showing their true colors.

I sincerely believe that their intentions were to protect me and not harm me. But though they were not consciously aware of their own protection mechanisms, their fears turned into subtle sabotage of me, which was the exact same thing as pouring strychnine into my coffee.

I remember leaving my very first large national convention—the one that spurred me on to starting my own coaching business. I was fired up because I had finally realized my purpose, seen my vision, and heard my calling.

I knew I was at a pivotal moment in my life. I knew that if I moved forward with my business, and if I was successful, I could create an incredible legacy for my family. We could afford the medications and nutritious foods we'd need to get healthy. We'd be able to rely on ourselves and create our own happiness. I felt like I had finally found the pot of gold at the end of the rainbow.

The first thing I did was to visit a mentor of mine who I respected immensely. She had taken me in when she didn't have to, taught me new skills I needed, and invested a disproportionate amount of time in my wellbeing and career. She had become my trusted advisor and confidant.

I remember sitting in her home at her kitchen counter, still energetic and ecstatic about what had happened at the conference. I told her that I was a little crab stuck in the bucket, but I had a new plan for how to get out and finally be *free.*

I still remember her response to this day, like a cold glass of ice dumped down my back: "I'd be really careful about going down that road. I've never seen anything like that work. You'd be better off staying at your comfortable, secure, *safe* job."

That was her advice! From this mentor whom I trusted to steer my life in lucrative and affirming new directions. Thankfully, I decided not to follow it, and instead I learned a valuable lesson. *Not all advice, even from people who love and care about you, is good advice.*

Sometimes people can't help but speak from their own fears and insecurities, and those things will not do you any good.

"DON'T BE COACH JAMIL."

I had a good friend I had known since the sixth grade, and we still got together on a fairly regular basis. However, when I started to make the shifts and decisions that would radically change my life and the lives of those in my family and inner circle, he grew very uncomfortable.

Whenever we hung out, he would say, "I don't want to be around Coach Jamil—I want the old Jamil, the one I knew in high school."

But—fortunately for me, and unfortunately for him—I wasn't the same person I had been ten or twenty years ago. I had grown, changed, and matured. I wasn't the same Jamil I had been in high school, and *that was a good thing*!

When you begin to follow your purpose and live out your vision, the fact is *you are going to change fundamentally.* And the people around you aren't always going to like it. They may complain that you're not your old self or that you're not the person you used to be. Changes that seem positive to you may seem scary and foreign to them. Your new mindsets may clash with their old belief systems.

And, whether intentionally or not, they may begin to make you feel guilty for changing, leaving them behind, and "abandoning" them.

But if you are committed to fulfilling your dreams, if you're excited about creating new things beyond the horizon, then *it's impossible for you to stay where you're at.* You have to put your foot down. You *have* to grow.

DON'T BE A POSER

I went on a vacation with some friends in Hawaii recently, and every once in a while, I would take a break from the activities to work on my business. My friends constantly hounded me: "You're not gonna *work* while you're on vacation, are you, Jamil?" and "You're not going to do any training calls while we're out here, right, Jamil?"

I know my friends love me and care about me, and they even want me to succeed in my business. But they didn't understand that *I was doing what I had committed to doing for my business and myself.* They didn't realize they were dumping strychnine into my coffee.

A few months later, I found myself in Costa Rica on a boys' trip. From time to time, I would go back into my room to study, train, and check in with clients.

Again, I met the same sentiment from my friends: "Jamil is changing, bro. He's too good to hang out with us," and "Oh, Jamil, you're not gonna *work*, are you? Man, I remember when you used to be *fun*."

My response was to shrug and say, "Okay."

In a way, I understood. I was striving for something they didn't see or understand. I was acting differently, and it made them uncomfortable. But I was doing what I wanted to do. What I was excited to do. What I had committed to doing: achieving my vision and elevating myself, my business, my life, and the lives of others around me to a new place.

Here's the deal: there's always a price to be paid. There will always be challenges in your way, and it just so happens that some of those challenges will come from people who love you. That doesn't mean they're bad people. They just don't understand that you are not the same.

But to graduate from grade one to grade two, you're going to have to learn to deal with issues and hurt and frustration from other people—including close friends, mentors, and family members—in your tribe. They will challenge you, and they may even fight you on certain matters. They will try to drag you back down to grade one. It's up to you to decide how to respond.

They said, "Count the cost."

— THINK LIFE *is* DIFFERENT

If you don't want to be fat anymore, your fat friends will still invite you out for Dodger Dogs. If you don't want to be poor anymore, your friends who are bad with money will still invite you with them to the casino. If you want to improve your marriage, your decision to stop going to strip clubs with your friends is going to impact them. (Hint: they're not going to like it.)

In some way or other, those closest to you will try to throw strychnine in your coffee.

Here's the hard truth: either your loved ones are going to step it up and come with you, or they're going to try and drag you back down with them into the crab bucket.

Regarding those who try to drag you back down into the crab bucket—if you truly want to grow and become more, you are going to have to leave those people behind. Now, you don't have to stop loving them. But you will need to have a game plan in place for if (and when) they try to drag you back down into the bucket.

Because people who oppress others never give up without a fight.

EMPATHY, LOVE, AND UNDERSTANDING

It's good to remember that the people around you love you and are trying to do what they believe is best for you. Even if they are dumping strychnine into your coffee or standing in the way of you accomplishing your dreams, they probably mean well. They're simply acting out of their best intentions, however uninformed those intentions may be.

So how do you deal with this issue? You have to prepare yourself and anticipate the sabotage before it begins.

Think about the president of the United States. Before jumping into a tough or complicated situation, he or she is briefed about whatever issues are about to go down so that they can formulate a response before anything happens.

We need to do the same thing—we need to brief you beforehand.

Before you break the news to your husband that you want to quit your job to start your own business, you will need to understand your husband's state of mind. Chances are he's not ready for you to spring this information on him. Chances are he hasn't been asking for massive change to come along and disrupt his life.

And chances are he cares about you a lot and does not want to see you get hurt.

All of those things he's feeling—fear, uncertainty, scarcity, and love—can get mixed up into a pretty potent cocktail that can lead to fights, hurt feelings, and worse. This is especially true if you fight fire with fire—if you respond to his fear reaction with a fear reaction of your own. Getting defensive, asserting loudly that you're right, screaming, fighting … that's not the way to go.

But if you understand all of that going in, you can intentionally bring empathy, love, and understanding to the discussion when it occurs. Just brief yourself beforehand. Use empathy to put yourself into his shoes and understand what your news may cause him to feel. Prepare yourself to navigate him through the talk with love and grace.

And don't take it personally if he's not immediately on board. I mean, if he immediately cheers you on, that's fantastic (and very rare). But more often than not, you will meet some resistance.

I know this sounds really difficult and unpleasant. But it's necessary if you want to change, grow, and level up in life. It might help if you look at it as a test—a challenge being brought up by those closest to you. Like any hero on a journey, you need to pass tests to get the things you want.

You can also look at it as a fantastic opportunity to practice your leadership skills and virtues. Give eternal grace, act out of love and a sense of service, and exercise empathy, patience, kindness, and understanding. These are values that you will need to begin to hold sacred.

THE INVISIBLE LINE OF BEING

In life, there's a mysterious, invisible line of being. And you're either above it or below it.

Above the line are all of the things which we know to be good and true. These are the positive things—openness, curiosity, a willingness to learn, a delight in helping and motivating others, and an optimistic mentality that "the glass is half full."

The people who are above the line are the big thinkers and doers, the encouragers, the motivators, the people who say, "No problem!" when you ask them for help. They react out of love.

Below the line are limiting beliefs, negative mindsets, fear, closed-mindedness, and the need to control others or be right all the time.

The people who are below the line are the complainers, the takers, the de-motivators, the people who talk about others behind their backs, the people who are terrified of risk and comfortable being comfortable. They react out of fear.

Now, being above the line and being below the line are both normal in the spectrum of human behavior. You're not a bad person if you spend time in both places! But the question is … do you *want* to?

Seven years ago, I lived below the line. I didn't know it at the time, but I was making a conscious decision to live there based on not only my own limiting beliefs and mindset but the people I was hanging around.

Like Jim Rohn said back in Shift Three, "You are the average of the five people you spend the most time with." If those people are all living below the line … guess where you're going to be? And if you manage to climb above the line despite them, chances are they're going to reach up and pull you right back down into the crab bucket.

This one took me a long time to finally understand, but … I finally realized I had to evaluate the people I was spending time with. I had to make a *conscious decision* about who I wanted to be and who I wanted to influence me. I had to make yet another shift and learn that it is still possible to love, honor, and understand people—and choose not to be around them (at all or as much).

There's no getting around it—*this is extremely hard.*

I had a really good friend (whom we'll call Lisa to protect the innocent) who had lived her entire life below the line. She and I were fantastic friends, and even though I was evolving and making a lot of new changes in my life, I wanted to preserve the friendship. I would drive hours to meet her on her own turf and try my hardest to listen, empathize, and connect. But it wasn't easy.

One day, we decided to go on a walk through a nature preserve, and as usual, Lisa steered the conversation below the line. She had a lot of distaste for the business I was in and one of my business partners in particular. She went on a rant about something this business partner had posted to Facebook, and that's when I was forced to evaluate the health of our friendship.

Lisa was extremely smart and had several advanced degrees. She personally valued education, correct spelling and grammar, and thoughtful discourse. My business partner, on the other hand, only had an eleventh-grade education at best.

As Lisa went on about this poor, innocent dude's misuse of semicolons, I tried my best to defend him. I told her that he had gotten into the coaching business to better his life and others' lives and that he had found incredible success doing so. I told her that she hadn't seen all of the people he was helping or the lives he was impacting on a daily basis, so it wasn't fair to judge his worth as a human being based on his spelling and grammar.

But Lisa just wouldn't drop it. She was having too much fun insulting him and dragging everyone below the line with her. She was the academic elite with multiple degrees, and my business partner was the equivalent of a beggar in the streets. And for some reason, she desperately needed me to know this.

They said, "Mind your own business. Most people don't have much because they're minding other people's business instead of their own."

— THINK LIFE *is* DIFFERENT

As she continued to cruelly berate him, I simply found myself thinking, "Jamil … some friends have got to go."

Some people don't get it and don't *want* to get it. And that's their choice. I still love Lisa, and I wish the best for her, but I choose not to spend time with her.

It's not just Lisa; I have *many* friends who are like this. "You still coaching fat people?" they'll ask with a judgmental snicker. Now, I know these people love me and care about me, even though they refuse to understand or value the work I do. So, I spend less time with them, if any. I set those boundaries so that I can continue to grow. I don't get dragged with them back into the crab bucket.

You can love people and still choose not to be around them.

SETTING BOUNDARIES AND SHUTTING DOORS

It's hard to set boundaries, shut doors, and separate yourself from people with whom you have a history. But it is also extremely necessary. Just like drug addicts have to leave their neighborhoods, and alcoholics need to find a new way home from work that doesn't take them past the bar, sometimes you need to get away from toxic people and places.

When I was growing up, all of my uncles were homeless except one. My mother used to invite them to live in our garage, so they wouldn't have to sleep in the street. But whenever my uncles would leave the streets to live with my mother, the rest of their buddies on the streets would say, "Where are you trying to go? You think you're better than us?"

It may be tempting to give in to the other crabs in the bucket and respond, "Who, me? Oh, I wasn't going anywhere." It is certainly easier to let yourself get pulled back in. But sometimes you need to put your foot down and stand up for your new life.

Because the cost of not bettering yourself, climbing above the line, and pursuing your dream is *real*. The consequences of letting yourself fall back down into the bucket are enormous. Nothing good comes of dreams deferred, let me tell you. You owe it to yourself, your family, your tribe, and more to discover your purpose and lean into it.

How many other people out there are relying on *you* to change their lives? How much good needs to be done in the world by your hand? What sort of impact are you depriving people of by playing it safe and denying your dream?

Leaving your tribe will certainly cost you.

But so will staying in the wrong one.

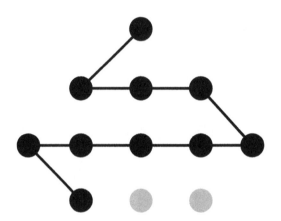

Shift Ten

Find Your Twelve

"If you want to go fast, go alone. If you want to go far, go together."

– AFRICAN PROVERB

What do Jesus, Jay-Z, Harriet Tubman, and Ray Kroc have in common? They have (or had) a *Find Your Twelve* mentality—your next superpower. They saw how life could be different, not just for themselves but for the world.

If they only did what they did for themselves, we wouldn't even know their names. They would be lost to history. Changing their lives for themselves would have been good. But we consider these people great. The question is why?

Let me share their secret right away: they had an abundance mentality. They were able to serve more people who served more people. Like an avalanche of change, their tiny bit of momentum swelled into gigantic movements that shaped the world as we know it. This is true in every arena. From religion to entertainment, from selling food to setting people free, each of these legendary leaders saw something so much bigger than themselves that it required they bring many along for the ride.

Allow me to explain.

THE TRICKLE-DOWN EFFECT

Recently, a friend reached out, asking for feedback on a business idea. When we spoke, she described her vision for a new kind of daycare that would help disadvantaged folks. The idea had burned in her heart for the past eight years, and she felt like now was the time to act. But she wanted some feedback and direction first.

After listening to her vision, I said, "That is amazing. One daycare is amazing—but have you considered opening thirty or forty?"

Silence.

She wasn't expecting that. But for many people I've coached over the years, this is the response. When the mission is multiplied ten, twenty, or thirty times, their mind reels at the magnitude of two things: what could be and what it will take to get there.

The problem is that my friend had been taught all of her life to open up one daycare. And don't get me wrong, that's a good thing; she will help people, serving twenty at a time. It is *good*, but it isn't *great*. When the mission is multiplied, she moves from serving twenty people to five hundred. That is truly *great*.

She has been thinking, praying, and planning this for eight years. So, I fully believe this is part of her purpose. However, thinking small—about the one—does not stem from an abundance mindset, which thinks about the many.

An abundance mindset doesn't ask, "How can I start one that will care for a handful of people and meet my family's needs?" An abundance mindset asks, "How can I start one thousand, and create opportunity for thousands?"

A multiplied mission taps into what I call the trickle-down effect, which is the bedrock impact of abundance. You see, successfully starting forty daycares begins first in her mind and depends on how big she sees the future. She cannot think small. Finding your twelve starts in the mind and is created in the world. When you think it, the people must come into place to make it come true. It requires that she finds dozens of people to bring alongside her. Picture the difference between thinking small and thinking abundantly like the following image.

In Figure A, one person is serving twenty people plus her family. This is good. In Figure B, one person is leading hundreds, giving them an opportunity to fulfill their purposes, care for their family, and change the lives of thousands. This is abundance at work.

THINKING BIGGER, BECOMING MORE

Have you ever heard of a man named Henry Box Brown? If you're like most, the answer is no. He was a slave in Virginia who made a genius plan to escape to freedom. In 1849, he mailed himself in a wooden crate to abolitionists in Philadelphia. I'm so inspired by people like him who didn't give up and found ways to achieve a better life. This is good.

Now, let me ask you about another person. Have you ever heard of Harriet Tubman? Of course you have! Her story is in history books,

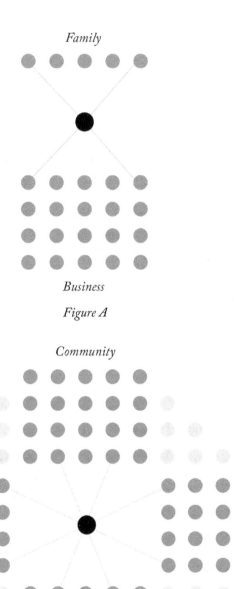

Family

Business

Figure A

Community

Family

Friends

Business

Figure B

on TV, and even in movies. Like Henry Box Brown, Harriet escaped from slavery to Philadelphia. But after finding a path to freedom, she did something different. *She went back.* She willingly risked her life and new-found liberty to free her fellow slaves, making thirteen perilous missions and starting what we now know as the Underground Railroad. Through-out her life, she led hundreds to safety and better lives. This is great.

Harriet saw something so much bigger than her own freedom. Her mindset was on a radically different level than most people, and because of her incredible vision, she had to build a network of safe houses and supporters in absolute secrecy. You see, the Underground Railroad was made of more than Harriet sneaking slaves in the night. It was a shared mission that required her to find her twelve. What she envisioned was so big, so audacious, that she recruited (and attracted) other brave souls to her cause. The mindset was the difference. And it's why we still marvel at her to this day.

You see, abundance forces you to become more. You must rise to the level of the mission, rather than the mission falling to your current level. So, how big do you want to see your life? How big a mission are you pursuing? And perhaps the greatest test is this: does the magnitude of your mission require you to become more and build an army of people marching shoulder-to-shoulder with you?

I first learned this lesson when I started my coaching practice. My mentors helped me see immediately that it's bigger than me. I wasn't in the business of helping one person at a time. While that was good, it was not great. I was in the business of reproducing myself in many who will help many more. My job was to trigger the trickle-down effect. Instead of focusing on meeting my own needs, I would focus on creating a thousand opportunities for many to change their lives.

This has proven true: if you give people what they want, you will get what you want. But by thinking bigger, you must become more. When I made and embraced this shift, everything changed. It will be the same for you. I prove this to those in our coaching family all the time through one of my favorite training exercises.

Imagine one hundred coaches sitting together in an auditorium. I ask for two volunteers. Hands shoot up throughout the crowd, and I pick two people, both equally capable and valuable. I instruct them to walk to the back of the auditorium and stand on opposite sides. Then, I give each the same task—with a slight twist.

I ask the first coach to walk into the crowd and bring back one other person. Then, I ask them to do that again and again, bringing back one person at a time. He or she builds a small tribe of people. *This is good.*

At the same time, I have the second coach go bring one person back as well. But here's the twist. Instead of touching one new person at a time on his or her own, the new members of their tribe also go bring one person back with them. So, one turns into two, two turns into four, four turns into eight, eight turns into sixteen, and so on.

By the end of the exercise, everyone in the audience is in one group or the other. But take an easy guess whose group is bigger. The second coach will often have ten times the number of people gathered as the first. *This is great.*

You see, our true superpower isn't in our own ability to accomplish a worthy mission. Our true superpower is reproducing our superpower in others because we've realized an abundant vision, a gigantic dream, and see something so much larger than ourselves that it takes an army to accomplish it.

No one does anything truly great without help. Even famous celebrities and stars who appear to stand alone—the tennis champion, the fashion designer, the pop star at center stage—even *they* have teams. They have managers, nutritionists, towel guys, makeup artists, medical personnel, trainers, coaches, psychologists, PR people, agents, friends, parents, siblings, cousins, and tons more.

Have you ever noticed that when someone wins an Oscar, Emmy, or Grammy, they don't always go up on stage alone? Or, if they do, they stand there for what seems like fifteen minutes listing out what feels like hundreds of names? Those are their teams. These famous individuals would not be there on stage without each and every one of those other people.

They said, "Give up the good for the great. Sacrifice now for a lifetime of freedom."

— THINK LIFE *is* DIFFERENT

I was successful on my own. But not nearly as successful as I became when I found my twelve. The most successful people I've ever met will tell you the same. The bigger the vision, the bigger the mindset, the bigger the team.

THE CARPOOL PHILOSOPHY

As we discussed in a previous shift, we as humans are genetically hardwired to form groups and tribes. There are just so many advantages to having a team that it's almost a waste of time, money, and energy to attempt anything meaningful on your own.

Think about driving on the freeway by yourself. Sure, you'll get from Point A to Point B, and along the way, you can pick whatever radio station you want to listen to. But you're currently stuck in traffic, while over in the carpool or HOV (high-occupancy vehicle) lane, cars full of two, three, four, or more people are zooming past you.

This is a fantastic analogy for all the benefits of finding your twelve and having more of an abundance mindset.

With your twelve, you get special access to the carpool lane, which allows you to get where you're going faster. It's more efficient, too, since you're also paying less per person for fuel, *and*, as a bonus, each person saves wear and tear on their own vehicle.

People who carpool (and have a carpool philosophy) also tend to have less stress, as instead of driving every day, you get to spend time reading, listening to music, or conversing with your carmates. Or, if you spend the nondriving time calling clients or catching up on email, you can boost your productivity, which is an extra bonus. And it has a far smaller impact on the environment.

Okay, so I don't know if teamwork is necessarily better for the environment. But all of those other carpooling benefits are also true of finding your twelve.

I know, it feels good to be able to leave the house whenever you want to and not have to pick anyone else up. It's *nice* to have that degree of control and flexibility. It suits our individualistic desires. It might even be working well for you right now. But that control, flexibility, and individualism will keep you stuck in the slow lane when it comes time to grow your business or life beyond what one person can feasibly do.

Because as much as we don't want to admit it, as individuals, we are incredibly limited. Even if you're only sleeping two or three hours a night (which I do *not* recommend), you can still only answer so many emails, take so many phone calls, and spend time with so many clients. There's only so much you can do around the house, paying bills, washing dishes, being there for all the kids, planning outings, and making arrangements. There are only so many hours in a day, and one person can only do so much.

I know—on the surface, all this talk of teamwork seems like a contradiction to what we learned in Shift Two, "Do Your Own Pushups." But I'm not talking about getting others to do your work *for* you or relying on someone else to take responsibility on your behalf. I'm talking about expanding your potential and your effectiveness. I'm talking about a magic word, and that word is *scale*.

We've all seen goldfish in a round fishbowl. They swim innocently about, eating their food, staring at their reflection, and probably wondering what all of those weird fish with arms and legs are doing outside of the water. But did you know that a goldfish only stays small when it lives in a bowl? They grow according to the size of their container. So, when a goldfish is introduced to a pond, they get larger—*even one hundred times larger*.

Just like goldfish, our mind is the container of our life. How big we grow is directly dependent on its expansiveness (or limitations). Are you content with a fishbowl life? A pond life? Or do you want to master the sea? The ocean offers unlimited potential, unexplored territory, and room for millions. And it is on the sea that you *must* scale. It's not simply that you *want to*, it's that you *have to* in order to accomplish your mission.

You see, a find-your-twelve mentality will force you to build a team and give you the power to *scale* in the process. This is where the true superpower lies.

When you have your twelve, you can expand and multiply yourself. You are no longer limited by the constraints of one individual—in fact, there are virtually no limits to the number of people you can bring with you. So, form a carpool and get in the fast lane—let's find your twelve.

YOUR VIBE ATTRACTS YOUR TRIBE

As we discussed in Shift Nine, the people around you can either accentuate or hinder your growth. Some people have your best interests at heart (like the disciple Peter) or hinder your growth (like Judas) by misguided actions. But other people simply do not want you to grow.

I've seen this happen countless times in my occupation as a coach. I've seen how the success of one partner in a marriage can swiftly reveal the insecurity in the other. I've seen friends who support you when you're stuck in your comfortable safe box, but the moment you begin to climb out, their applause quickly dies.

These are obviously not the people you want with you.

In 2013, I began studying Rumi intensively. He says, "Set your life on fire and seek those who fan your flames." If the people you are considering for your team do *anything* but fan the flames when you light your fire, *they are not the right people for your team.*

If they run from the flames, if they hide from it behind traditions and norms and antiquated concepts, if they attempt to douse the fire … walk away. These are not the right people for your team, and you run the very real danger of allowing their insecurities to define you and your business and limit your success.

Similarly, if *you're* the one who's insecure, frightened, ego-driven, hiding behind old customs and norms, or actively running away from the fire, I encourage you to change. I often say that your vibe attracts your tribe—that is, like attracts like. Strength attracts strength, just as weakness attracts weakness.

They said with intensity, "YOU DON'T GET PEOPLE TO DO ANYTHING. FIND OUT WHAT THEY WANT AND HELP THEM GET IT."

— THINK LIFE *is* DIFFERENT

If you want to start encouraging the right people to find you and become part of your twelve, you must act like the strong, fire-fanning people you want to attract.

HOW DO YOU LEAD YOUR TWELVE?

I want to be clear—I'm not saying that you can't be successful on your own. I'm just saying you'll be a hell of a lot more effective with your twelve because an *abundant* vision mandates you have them. But leading isn't exactly easy—it takes a lot of hard work and intentionality, it takes time, and it often takes a couple of missteps. However, it *is* worth it.

The first thing you'll want to do is to find people who believe what you believe. Find the values you prize and the virtues you extol. Most of all, find people who want to make a crazy impact on the marketplace, just like you do.

In my life and business, the values I look for in my twelve are:

1. **Integrity.** *I need to know that I can trust and rely on them, whether I'm around or not. People who I know will do what they say they're going to do.*

2. **Personal responsibility.** *I want people who do their own pushups and who are intrinsically motivated to do the work.*

3. **Competence.** *I want people who do the work and do it well, and who have the superpowers that complement mine.*

4. **Good people and leadership skills.** *I want people who can both listen carefully and rally the troops when the time comes.*

5. **A heart for service.** *I look for people who genuinely want to serve—the business, their partners, the mission, and the vision.*

I want my twelve to have these values even though their superpowers and gifts may all be different. But these are the non-negotiables.

You may even find that you need multiple teams of "twelve" to help you find and maximize success. For example, I have a financial team, a direct sales team, a book team, a marketing team, and a team in our house to make sure everything runs smoothly. My financial team is made up of my financial advisors, portfolio managers, accountants, and more.

My direct sales team comprises truly amazing coaches who have a carpool philosophy and uphold the important values and virtues we find important. And my home team is made up of Amanda, who supports me and raises our children while managing the house, and also includes our nannies, my personal assistant, and additional house managers who cook, clean, and do laundry.

Not doing everything yourself *doesn't make you lazy*. I know that's a mindset that a lot of us can easily fall into. But it's a trap. When you delegate things that aren't in your wheelhouse or skillset to someone who can do it more quickly and easily, you free yourself to work on the things *you* are specially equipped to work on. You live toward your purpose. They live toward *their* purpose. Your business, life, and impact grows. You help more and more people and give more and more value to the world. Everybody wins. By the way, life, just like the freeway, has a funny way of rewarding those with a carpool philosophy and an abundance mindset.

Now, let's address the elephant in the room. You may be thinking, *there's no way I can afford to build my team of twelve!* I submit to you: before my mindset got really big, I couldn't afford those things either. And if you don't have a find-your-twelve mentality, you're right, you probably can't afford it. But when you take on a find-your-twelve mindset, you'll be amazed at how everything changes. Your lack is probably because you're focused primarily on earning for yourself. You're thinking about how you can eat instead of how you can help others eat. But when you elevate your mindset, just watch what happens. If you want to blow yourself away, think bigger than yourself.

Once you find your twelve, you'll have to spend a majority of your time off the bat working with them, mentoring them, and training them up. But once you have them up and running … look out, world.

BE READY TO CHANGE

Your twelve will not always stay the same. Some members will leave voluntarily, and others will leave because you need to change your roster. Just like sports teams are different every year, your teams will shift, grow,

They said, "Even JESUS had a team. Why would you waste time trying to do it on your own? Who will your twelve be?"

— THINK LIFE *is* DIFFERENT

and change along with you and your life and business needs. You may outgrow or outpace certain members, and that's okay.

The accountant you hire when you're just starting out as a small business will probably not be the same accountant you are using ten years later when you add in assets, properties, and millions in revenue. At that time, you may want someone who is more aggressive and dynamic and less risk averse.

Whether it's an assistant, attorney, accountant, house manager, business partner, or someone else entirely, you will need people on your team who are on the same wavelength as you. And that wavelength is subject to change based on where you are in life and where your business is and needs to be.

As you move from stepping-stone to stepping-stone, your team may need to change, and that is okay. Sometimes Judas has to go. But hey, eleven out of twelve ain't bad. This is important because if you hold on to the wrong people, you may be holding yourself back—and holding them back too.

FIND YOUR TWELVE

Now, let's revisit the life of someone you may have heard of—Jesus of Nazareth. One day, it dawned on me that, in terms of his model of leadership, he never tried to go it alone. God put a big task in front of him. Plus, he had a clock counting down, having only three years. So, he must've thought it would be rather silly to try and accomplish this mission all on his own. So, he began to find his twelve. He went from region to region, searching for people who wanted more—and knew they were made for it.

What was Jesus trying to teach us (directly or indirectly)? On the surface, this seems to be all about building a team so you can grow and move faster. Many hands make light work, right? However, there is a deeper meaning. It's about building a team so *they* can grow faster. As a leader, you become the creator of opportunities.

At the first convention I went to, I started hearing about these people who were earning abundantly.

I asked, "How long have these people been coaching?" Most who I asked about had been coaching for five years, six years, eight years, ten years ... I went back to my room and wondered, "How are all these people doing better than me economically? I have been out of college and working for nine years, while the majority of them have been working for less time. What is going wrong here? What's the difference?"

The difference was trying to do it by myself.

Before I started coaching, I'd spent too much of my life trying to go it alone. I quickly learned that if you want to go fast, go by yourself. But if you want to go far, find your twelve. Shortly after, I understood that this shift didn't just apply to my business; it applied to every area of my life as well.

Today, some things have changed. My mindset isn't just to chop down a single tree but to chop down a forest.[1] Now, if I have to chop down a forest, the first thing I'm going to do is find twelve of the biggest, baddest dudes. Why would I spend my whole life trying to chop down a forest by myself? Even if I do that, and there's a huge pile of gold at the end of it, I'm going to be exhausted, unable to enjoy it, and will have failed to help anyone else in the process.

TOM SAWYER

That's what people do in our economy. They spend forever working, building, and pushing alone, all to retire at age sixty-five. They only have a little bit of time to enjoy whatever they were working toward and hopefully, kids who talk to them. Instead, we need an economy filled with Tom Sawyers.

Remember Mark Twain's classic novel, *The Adventures of Tom Sawyer* (Or maybe just the movie with Jonathan Taylor Thomas!) In the story, Tom needs to paint a fence white. That's a lot of long, tiresome work for one kid. So, what does he do? He recruits neighborhood friends to do it with him.

---

[1] Please note, I would never chop down a forest :).

This scene has always stood out to me because this is the mindset of a different kind of person. Who does he have to *BE* in order to go out and rally all these kids to come paint this fence? It's a big job—but he turns it into a big opportunity for everyone, not just himself. This is the shift; Tom Sawyer found his twelve, and it all started with his mindset.

DO YOU SEE HOW LIFE CAN BE DIFFERENT?

Seeing things bigger begins in our minds then flows into the world. It is also how you level up your self-perception. You see, I think there's more to you than you give yourself credit for. I'm here to tell you there's a reason you're reading this, and there's a reason that there are people you're thinking about right now. I never thought life could be different. We're not trained to think this way.

For example, my son is in the third grade. He's taught to take tests on his own. From a young age, he's already been taught to solve problems by himself. I don't want to do that. I don't want to be my own attorney, my own accountant, or my own mechanic.

When I have challenges, I'd rather go to my twelve to solve them together. Honestly, it just makes more sense. But from our earliest schooldays, we're not trained like that.

Simply put, this shift asks these questions over and over again:

- *"How do I make my superpower become theirs?"*

- *"How does my superpower unlock theirs?"*

- *"How do I create opportunities for their unique genius to shine?"*

- *"How do I multiply my mission to be so gigantic I couldn't possibly accomplish it on my own?"*

- *"How do I think life could be different?"*

JAY-Z

Another master of this mindset is Jay-Z, who, just like Jesus, found his twelve. When he got started in the music industry, he built a name for

They said, "Lean not on
your own understanding."

— THINK LIFE *is* DIFFERENT

himself. Jay-Z became a brand larger than life and was hungry to stand as one of the great hip-hop artists. Every time people talked about the best ever, he wanted his name in the mix.

Then he had to shift.

He had gone to the mountaintop and been relatively successful. Then he asked why he was only doing this for himself. Part of his mission was to make sure everyone could hear good music. This meant he would have to expand himself. After all, "everyone" is a lot of people. So, he worked tirelessly to teach, train, mentor, coach, and build a label of the best musicians in the industry today.

These are artists like Eminem and Kanye West. Musicians so successful Jay-Z got to say, "I done made more millionaires than the lotto did."

On his own, he was *good*. With his twelve, he is *great*. What he produced by himself pales in comparison to what he did once he started providing more value to more people through his label. He's served more great music to more people by creating abundant opportunities. He made his superpowers theirs.

LEAVE SCARCITY FOREVER

Trying to do everything on your own is living from a scarcity mindset. My friend dreamed of starting just one daycare, because she saw it small. Again, this is good. However, even good things can still grow from a scarcity mindset. To attain freedom, advance a huge mission, and building generational wealth requires an abundance mindset. The mindset of someone who is just looking out for their family makes that person miss the chance to better their whole community, country, and even the world.

Ray Kroc, the genius behind McDonald's, saw two brothers with a bustling hamburger and shake stand. The brothers were content with one restaurant serving hundreds of happy, sugared-up customers. But Kroc saw it so much bigger. He wasn't interested in serving hundreds; he was interested in billions. Today, decades later, McDonald's serves sixty-two million people *per day*.[2]

Finding your twelve is about *thinking big*. It's about being a leader. It's about growing yourself so big that you expand to the level of your mission. It's about becoming *so much more* than you are today that you never have to talk about yourself, because people around you will readily tell your story.

Jesus's self-assurance and belief in his grand mission to save the world was so powerful he didn't have to give long lectures to his disciples. He showed up, dropped a, "Follow me …," and led twelve ordinary men to turn the world upside down. This is because of *all that he was*. Again, who did he have to *be*?

To make this shift means to do more by doing less. It's not just thinking differently; it's thinking oppositely. It isn't about finding a ful-filling job; it's about creating *thousands of jobs* and building powerful teams of twelve to facilitate it. Finding your twelve is about understand-ing time freedom. Jesus often would seclude himself up on the mountain, and even when he wasn't "working," the mission was being accomplished. Jay-Z doesn't write every line for every artist. But even when he's sleep-ing, thousands of people listen to his label's music. Harriet Tubman didn't build every safe house. But at night, hundreds were harbored from danger.

How? They found their twelve. Your superpower is reproducing your superpower. Your impact becomes exponential when you reproduce it in others. But it takes a mission so large, so abundant, that you wouldn't dream of doing it on your own. So, I ask you … Do you have a mindset that allows you to see things so big, it requires you to find your twelve? And if you don't, I encourage you to adopt one *today*.

As Rumi says, "Yesterday I was clever, so I wanted to change the world. Today I am wise, so I am changing myself." Whether you've thought about it or not, this is how we change the world: one mind, one vision, and twelve people at a time.

---

[2] Badkar, Mamta. "18 Facts About McDonald's That Will Blow Your Mind." *Business Insider*, 20 Apr. 2012, www.businessinsider.com/19-facts-about-mcdonalds-that-will-blow-your-mind-2012-4

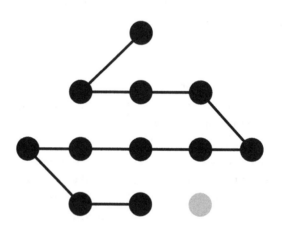

Your Goals Don't Give a Damn

"Pain pushes until vision pulls."

– DR. MICHAEL BERNARD BECKWITH

Listen. I care about you. Your mom cares. Your pastor cares. Your kids care. Your best friend cares. We all care. We will sit with you and listen to your excuses, moans, and limiting beliefs—probably forever. But do you know who doesn't care?

Your goals don't give a damn. The only thing they care about is that you suck it up and bring them into reality.

You see, your goals are just like your kids. You might be sick, but they don't care; they still want to eat. Your goals aren't concerned with your fear or desire for comfort. They just want you to get after it. They are part of a grand vision for life—a bigger life than you ever thought possible. And they're freaking excited, because now you've tapped into something that's magnificent. They've laid dormant—but now can be realized. They've been hidden in the dark—but their purpose is to come into the light.

As you read this, they're throwing little goal parties, salsa dancing, and celebrating. They're screaming, "We've been locked in here for thirty-two years, and this person is finally gonna let us out!" They are ready for you to become stronger and *quit wimping out.*

Remember, your friends will placate you. Rub your back. Caress your hand. Sink into the pit with you and commiserate. But you know who doesn't give a damn?

Your goals!

Right now, you're on step two of twenty-four. If you want to get to step three, it's time to graduate through some things. Here's what it looked like for me: When I felt like I didn't have enough time, I had to break through. When Amanda left for two weeks, saying our marriage was over, I had to get stronger. When it seemed like no clients were ready to join me, I had to read some more books. When all my coaches were leaving, it was time to dig down deep inside and repeat the process.

My friend, the point of this chapter is simple. I care about you, the people around you care, your mom cares, and God cares—and we care enough to listen to every excuse in the book. But do you know who doesn't care?

Your goals don't give a damn.

Now, you can't know what thoughts or actions are serving you in your quest to achieve your goals and higher vision. That's why it's time to measure them against what you truly want. But if you don't know, you can't judge them. One of my earliest dreams was that everyone from Temple City, California, where I grew up, to Long Beach, where I live now, would find physical health. So, I began to judge my thoughts and actions by this desire. But what about you?

I ask again, what do you want?

Pretend that there's no one around to judge, tear down, destroy, or dismiss your response (like there was in Shift Nine). All of those toxic people are gone. Your circumstances don't matter right now. What's strictly "possible" doesn't matter, either. You can really let yourself think big and dream bigger.

Ask yourself: What do I *want?*

Maybe you're thinking, "I want to earn $10,000 a month." It may feel silly or outlandish to you, but say it anyway. Taste the words. Really make those words—and the thoughts behind them—feel *real*.

Ask yourself: why do you want to earn $10,000 a month? What would it mean for you? How would it feel? How would your life change? What would you be free to do and accomplish? Imagine all of those things. Envision yourself in this situation. Really let yourself feel the feelings that would accompany a $10,000 per month paycheck.

Similarly, what would happen if you *didn't* earn $10,000 a month? This one might be easier to envision, especially if it's the reality you're living now. What would you miss out on? What would you not be free to do and accomplish? How does this make you feel?

Lean back into those feelings of earning $10,000 per month, and—just for a moment—allow yourself to imagine what it might feel like to make $30,000 per month. What would that mean for you? How would it feel? How would it change your life? What would you be free to do and accomplish?

What happens if you bump that number up to $60,000 per month? Or $100,000 per month?

If you're not familiar with this process, what we're doing right now is called *visioning*. And it's one of the most important things you can do for your business or for your life. You can replace the $10,000 a month with happiness, joy, peace, a healthy marriage, a new job, a physique that inspires you, anything, as long as it's truly important to you.

I grew up poor, and as I was growing up, it was better if I didn't want things. I wasn't going to get the things I wanted, so if I didn't want them, I wouldn't get hurt when I didn't get them. From new toys to sports equipment to a Nintendo Game Boy, I simply learned that I couldn't have everything I wanted. We couldn't afford it. And that was it.

But we've been through Shift Three, and we've learned to start asking, "How can I afford this?" We've learned that we're allowed to want things. The next step is naming the things that you now want.

So … what do you *want*? What do you want for yourself, your family, and your business (or job)? What do you want for your life now and in the future? In the next five years, what do you want to *do*? What do you want to create? What would blow your mind financially? Why do you want these things? And what would it mean to get them? How would it feel?

What about the next *ten* years? What do you want to do, create, make, and become within that time frame? Why do you want these things? What would it mean to receive, earn, and accomplish them? How would it *feel*?

Over the course of your life, what do you want for your business?

What do you want for yourself physically?

Mentally?

Spiritually?

Relationally?

… And *why*?

They said, "My son,
I promise, if you do more
than you're paid to do,
eventually you'll be paid
far more than what you do."

─ THINK LIFE *is* DIFFERENT

How would you *feel* if you got these things?

How would you feel if you *didn't*?

What is at stake? What do you have to gain? To lose? What were you born to do? What is your purpose? Whom are you supposed to become? Is what you're doing right now all you have in you? Or are you supposed to be doing *more*? Come on … be truthful. What is it you *want*?

YOUR GAME PLAN FOR GETTING WHAT YOU WANT

There is no limit to what you can envision for yourself. And, with the right game plan, there is no limit to making everything you envision a reality.

Spend some quality time answering the questions in the previous section about what you *want*. Set a timer and type it out, journal it, or whiteboard it, either alone or with members of your team. Just be sure that when you're done, *you know what you want*. In my book, *The Richest Man in Direct Sales*, I talked about how becoming financially successful is *easy* to do. The problem is: it's easier *not* to do. What I just suggested is *easy* to do. But truth be told, most people won't do it because it's simply easier not to do. It's easier not to spend a couple minutes and truly figure out what the hell they want.

Now, what *you* just came up with, that's your vision. Now it's time to ask a new set of questions, starting with: What actions are you going to take to produce this vision? And, what are you willing to give up to produce this vision? I'm sorry to be the bad guy, but your goals are possible; they just come with a caution sign, and that sign says, "You can have it, just not for free."

Because you won't reach these goals for free, you have to do your push-ups every single day. One strategy to make it easier is to work backward from the goal itself. So, if you want to make $30,000 per month, how is that going to happen? How many new clients or customers would you need to serve? How would you need to expand your team? What sort of revenue would be needed monthly? Annually? What new types of training would you require? What books would you need to read? Which people would you need to talk to?

As with so many other things, other people are often the key. In my case, when I realized what it was that I wanted, I found a mentor who had already accomplished it. She helped me to understand the steps I would need to take to get there, and she helped to guide me along the way.

It's also helpful to realize that *massive goals are not accomplished in a day.* Smaller goals may need to be reached first, habits may need to be changed, and chain reactions may need to take place. *You* will probably even need to change—your mindset, your habits, your daily activities, even the way you talk to people. It's your job to outline the game plan that will take you from point A to point Z and to realize all of the steps you will need to take along the way.

This may start with something as simple as a daily game plan. If there were five to ten things you could do every day that could start the chain reactions that will get you to point Z, what would they be? For instance, if I wanted to move from making $2,000 per month to $10,000 per month, my five daily actions might be:

1. *Eat well and exercise so that I can perform at my peak every day.*

2. *Find, and be in touch with, my mentor daily.*

3. *Decide how many people to talk to in order to to grow my business—and then double that number.*

4. *Spend a significant amount of time finding my twelve.*

5. *Never start the next day without already having it figured out on paper.*

This is just an example of a daily game plan. Your own daily game plan will change as you change and shift as you continue to make new shifts and drop old habits that no longer serve you. It's important to remember that your vision is fueled by emotion. Your game plan is made real through action. And each action should be done for a reason that supports your vision.

THE HIERARCHY OF WANTS

One of your latent superpowers is understanding what you *actually want*. Because when you can discern and understand what you *truly* want, you can build a game plan and begin turning those wants into realities.

Sometimes, you'll experience multiple wants that compete against each other. For example, say I want to lose weight, but I also want to eat a big, double-chocolate-chip brownie. I have two wants ... which will win?

- *I want to be financially independent, but I always want to spend my money on fun stuff and not invest it. Two wants ... which will win?*

- *I want to be an excellent husband (or wife), but I always want to be right. Two wants ... which will win?*

- *I want to create financial freedom, but I also want to work only twenty-five hours a week right now. Two wants ... which will win?*

- *I want to finish the project because the deadline is tonight, but I also want to binge the last four episodes of my favorite show on Netflix. Two wants ... which will win?*

- *I want to deepen my spiritual relationship with my Creator and lead a virtuous life, but I also really enjoy cheating on my spouse. Two wants ... which will win?*

- *I want to start a reading system in the evenings so that I can truly develop myself, but I'm often too tired to stay up and get the reading done. Two wants ... which will win?*

- *I want to build a large business that requires me to stay in town and attend a training, but I also want to go to a family reunion during that same time. Two wants ... which will win?*

I know the examples above seem childishly simple—obviously, if you have a project due at midnight, you should work on it and not indulge in watching Netflix until it's done. But these decisions are often *uncommonly difficult* to make in the moment. At the time, it's easier to choose the immediate gratification of a double-chocolate-chip brownie over the delayed gratification of losing weight.

"It's just this one time," we reason with ourselves. "Next time, I'll skip the brownie and have carrot sticks instead. I just deserve a little treat this time." But all of those "just this one time" events prevent the massive results we wish we could achieve.

This is where the need for discernment and the hierarchy of wants comes into play. Because it's not just about which choice you want. It's about which choice you want *more*. It's about which choice ultimately serves you and your vision.

If your vision is to lose weight, then foregoing the brownie is the right choice. It serves your higher vision. It may not make you happy now, but you will find the freedom later. But the decisions aren't always that obviously simple or even that small-scale. In fact, you may discover that you have *more than two massive wants that serve your vision. The question is which serves your higher vision?* This is very normal! And all of those massive wants, when fulfilled, will add up to the higher vision that you've always dreamed of.

For example, when I started my coaching business, I had big goals and visions. The type of goals that would force me to find my twelve. I wanted the meaning of the "Frazier" last name to forever change. I wanted to leave a positive legacy for my son Ezra, and have the ability to spend not just weekends with him doing fun activities, but months with him traveling the world if we wanted to. I wanted my family to have massive options for the rest of our lives. However, to get the business up and running required me to spend a tremendous amount of time working on it. This created conflict between these two desires. Ezra would have a game, one of his friends would have a birthday party, and Amanda's family would have a *quinceañera*. But at the same time, growing my business required me to lead (or attend) a training, meet with potential clients, or do any one of a million other things.

So now, I'd be in a bind. Two wants, two visions ... which would win?

I had to measure, which one did I want more? I could attend the birthday party, which would give immediate satisfaction. Or, I could build my business which would give us freedom forever. This delayed gratification would mean I wouldn't simply be happy for a weekend (or multiple weekends); we could be happy for a lifetime. Just like I could be happy in the moment, eating a double-chocolate-chip brownie, but if I didn't, in two months, I could have the physical freedom I was looking for.

Two wants ... which will win?

Do you want short-term satisfaction or long-term freedom? This is why I said, "You can have it, just not for free." To attain long-term freedom, you will need to pay the price of focusing on *just one want at a time*. Paying a price like this *will* become frustrating. You will want to quit, complain, throw in the towel, question if it's for you, or, more egregiously, question your Creator. You will want to make excuses, and you will have friends like me who will sit there and listen to your excuses. And you know why we'll do that? Because we care.

But ... your goals? They don't give a damn. All they want is to become realized. They know they can live. They know they can become true. They know they can experience the world, but it'll never happen until you dig deep, allow discomfort to be your best friend, make hard choices, delay gratifications, and start living in structure—and this is a powerful way to get everything you want out of life.

If I could be so bold to say, everything I just wrote is the *one* reason people are not as successful as they want to be. Going for the higher want again is easy to do, it'll just always be easier not to do.

For instance, let's say you're a mama who wants to stay home with your kids. Right now, you're working a full-time job, eight to ten hours per day, spending four hours every night with the kids (at best). This is killing you. Your kids are in daycare every day while someone else showers their philosophies on your children, when *you* want to be the one passing on your family's values and virtues.

So, your higher vision is to replace your income with your business in order to stay at home with your kids. This is a want. However, you would also prefer that your kids never spend time on their iPads or in front of the TV in the evening. This is another want. But in order to reach your higher vision, you will need to come home, make calls, do marketing, and build a business capable of replacing your income.

They said, "Don't start
tomorrow until it is
well planned."

— THINK LIFE *is* DIFFERENT

Two wants … *which will win?*

You could come home, not make calls, and spend those four hours with the kids. That's fine. But the frustration of having your kids in day-care will last for years. However, you could hire someone to watch them in your home, or even let them spend some screen time now, so you can work on the business for a year and reap decades of freedom.

It's a tough decision. But the choice I'm suggesting we each make is one that will fit our higher vision and wants. In this case, time freedom. This framework for living seems crazy if you want a normal existence. But if you want an abnormal existence, you'll need to make abnormal choices.

"PAIN PUSHES UNTIL VISION PULLS"

Through building my business, I never lost sight of my higher vision. Your higher vision is one of your most powerful tools, though many of us forget this.

As Dr. Michael Bernard Beckwith says: "Pain pushes until vision pulls." The pain surrounding your present circumstances will keep push-ing you toward success, until your vision finally catches hold of you and pulls you, like a giant, powerful dog on a leash, toward it.

My vision pulled me through all of the challenges, obstacles, mind games, frustrations, disappointments, fights, arguments, betrayals, and every other insane thing that happened throughout my journey. Things that would have stopped me in my tracks, were it not for my vision. Things that made me want to give up, quit, and go back to my "normal life."

Part of the vision that pulled me through the most difficult times was that of another man raising my son Ezra. That, more than anything, got me fired up to keep going. What would that other man be saying to Ezra? What would he teach him? Would Ezra build a bond with him that we didn't have? Would he have thoughts and belief systems that opposed mine? If my marriage didn't work out, what would another man shape my son to be?

They said, "Make sure
to leave an inheritance.
Not just for your kids,
but for your kids' kids."

— THINK LIFE *is* DIFFERENT

My vision kept me working hard—not only regarding what I *didn't* want (another man raising my son, a boss who constantly questioned my numbers, a "normal" life), but toward what I actively *wanted.*

I wanted a home that was larger than my 700-square-foot condo. I wanted to be thinner and feel better physically. At the beginning, I wanted to earn $18,000 per month. I wanted to do as I pleased with my free time. I wanted to be in the upper echelon.

There came a point where I didn't even necessarily want these specific things anymore—instead, I saw a place where I could be free every single day in every single way. My vision grew and matured out of a list of wants into a larger system—a new life in a new world. The promised land.

That vision of the promised land became so strong that it pulled me toward it. The sacrifices that I made for that vision hurt less. I was able to work harder and put in more sweat equity. I delayed my gratification just a little and then just a little more.

The vision was worth it.

EXPANDING YOUR VISION

Normal people have normal wants and make normal decisions based on their normal vision. But I think that if you're reading this book, you are not normal.

Many of us are guilty of having normal wants and visions. And many times, normal wants and visions are relatively *small* wants and visions, based off of the system in which we were raised or our current circumstances.

Maybe your vision is to make enough money to pay your rent and bills on time. Maybe your vision is to help your parents make house payments and buy the medicines they need. But let me ask you this: Is your current vision holding you back from what you could *really* achieve? Is your current vision so small it's actually *trapping* you into staying small? Are you striving for the bare minimum ... and nothing more?

What if, instead of simply paying your rent and bills on time, your vision was to buy a massive property on one hundred acres of land with *cash* and live debt free forever?

What if, instead of helping your parents with their payments and medications, you were able to pay off their house, move them into a top-notch assisted-living facility, and spend all of the quality time you wanted with them?

What if, instead of turning over the couch cushions for laundry money, you turned your annual income into your monthly income?

What would it look like if you expanded your vision? What if you knew you were the kind of person who could bring in massive income or affect enormous change in society? What kind of life do you *want* to live?

When you change and expand your vision, you will change and expand your wants and make new and different choices. You will actually grow to fit that vision, if you let yourself. You will begin to make decisions in line with higher and higher wants. You're not going to make "normal" decisions based on "normal" standards anymore.

Earning my first $1 million was relatively simple—but it was *believing I could actually do it* that was hard! To do that, I had to change my definition of myself from someone who struggled to pay rent to someone who could bring in massive income. And to do that, I had to change and expand my vision and make decisions accordingly.

The decisions weren't easy—there was a lot of delayed gratification (and I mean, *a lot*), and I have to admit, sometimes I may have looked a little weird to the "normal" people around me.

But I didn't want to be "normal." I didn't want to settle for normalcy anymore. So, when people stared, I didn't care. When they made fun of me for working on vacation, I shrugged and said, "Okay." I stopped watching my beloved Monday Night Football for six years. I stopped caring what people thought of me. I stopped judging myself by their "normal" standards. I stopped caring.

And when I made my first million, they stared even more, and I cared even less. I simply smiled, painted a new, even higher vision, and got back to work.

LIVING IN STRUCTURE

Okay, so how do we expand our game plan to support our expanding vision? We live in structure. Here's a practical example of how that works:

At one point in my life, I wanted to be in the top 1 percent of performers in my industry. I had an intense desire for this, and I got really inspired about the idea of being able to rise to that rank and create something truly amazing. I started to believe, like Neo, that what I wanted was not only possible but possible for me. Belief turned into knowing, and I was ready.

I have a list of ten things that I did to reach my goal of becoming that 1-percent performer:

1. ***I established a morning routine.*** *I woke up at 5:00 a.m., spent fifteen minutes in prayer, fifteen minutes in meditation, and focused on my ultimate goal. This didn't happen only on the days I felt like it—it happened every damn day.*

2. ***I asked for help from God.*** *(Or the Universe, whatever you wanna call IT). Just like finding my twelve, I needed help to achieve what I was after. We cannot achieve abundant dreams on our own—it takes a team and a higher power.*

3. ***I planned each day.*** *I never started with a blank calendar. Before the day started, I always knew who I would meet with, reach out to, and impact. Every coffee was scheduled and every task accounted for. I never began a day without already having lived it in my mind.*

4. ***I lived on my calendar.*** *If it wasn't on my calendar, it didn't exist. I planned my work then worked my plan. Setting appointments on a calendar isn't magic; taking consistent action is the secret sauce to success.*

5. ***I attracted ambassadors.*** *At minimum, I would share my story with ten people per day. They would understand my mission and what I was doing, and I would challenge them to come along. Whether one-to-one, on social media, or via text message, three-hundred people heard from me each month.*

They said, "It's not the number that counts; it's the plan that counts."

— THINK LIFE *is* DIFFERENT

6. *I set my social media calendar and built a branding plan.* *Every day, I would post six times: 6:00 a.m., 9:00 a.m., 12:00 p.m., 3:00 p.m., 6:00 p.m., and 9:00 p.m. Every three hours, I took a step toward building the brand I dreamed of.*

7. *I recruited potential business partners.* *Finding my twelve wasn't simply a goal; it was a necessity. Because my mission had become so much larger, I had to find my twelve. Tom Sawyer would've been proud.*

8. *I cared for my body.* *I practiced yoga. I walked the beach. I got massages.*

9. *I reached out to my mentor.* *At least three times per day, I checked in with my mentor, asking her if I was on the right track. This was about building a relationship by inviting her input and feedback. I respected her insight and wanted it every chance I could get.*

10. *I spent one hour in self-development.* *Enter my mental mentors. Every morning, my mind was fed by mentors like Rumi, Marcus Aurelius, Jim Rohn, Jesus, Gandhi, and more. Their words still play on repeat in my mind, forming me, shaping me, and guiding me to become more than I could have on my own.*

In all of this, my greatest power was consistency. And I learned a valuable lesson: it isn't hard to grow into the top 1 percent through diligence. When you have the right plan, and you take action on it every day, success becomes inevitable rather than impossible. My vision became a question of when, not if.

When you think about it, it's almost funny. We all have incredible superpowers, but so few use them. In this season, I learned to apply every shift and flex each superpower every day. I didn't always want to, but that was okay. I didn't have to want to; I simply had to choose to. Remember, my goals (and yours) don't give a damn—that's up to us.

DO IT ANYWAY

All of these steps are relatively simple, yes, but they require a lot of hard work, dedication, and sacrifice. Basically, there's going to be a *lot* to complain about.

Now, complaining has its place. Sometimes you just need to vent some steam. I get that. But it's incredibly easy to vent the pain, discomfort, and hardship through complaining when you should be channeling it into hard work and fuel for your goal.

Here's what I mean. Some people—often, those who live *above the line* that we discussed in Shift Nine—deal with their pain by taking action, doing something, and changing their situation. But some people—especially those who live *below the line*—deal with their pain by complaining, being negative, and dragging others into the crab bucket with them.

I find it interesting when people complain about their situation instead of changing or fixing it, especially after I give them a good starting point that they decide to ignore. Because while complaining is easy, taking action is hard.

The good news is that you're not stuck above or below the line forever. You can move from one place to the other. All it takes is a mindset shift and the decision to act on what you truly *want* for your life. Complaining and taking action both alleviate pain—one just happens to get better results.

Back in 2012, I was in a place where I had realized that my core wants and desires centered around creating a life where I wasn't constantly stressed out by my lack of finances. I also wanted a healthier marriage, body, and mind. I didn't want to be depressed anymore. I didn't want the bathroom scale to say 218 pounds anymore.

Wanting things to be different was easy. Complaining that I wanted things to be different was easy. Doing things to fix my situation and manifest my wants into reality … that was hard.

Up until that point, I only did things consistently if I *felt* like it. If my marriage was going well that day, or if I'd had a great week at work, or if I had what I felt like was a plethora of money in my account, the stars had aligned, and I didn't need to do any work.

But … the stars don't consistently align. Which meant that reaching and enjoying my goals was also inconsistent. Makes sense, right? But at the time, I couldn't envision working for what I wanted. I couldn't see living in a structured, purposeful way that would *cause* the stars to align.

The problem was that I was basing my life and my decisions off of emotions, not structure.

Case Study One

At one point, my mentor asked me, "What do you want, Jamil?"

Me: "A happy marriage, to lose weight, a life without stress, freedom over my time, and financial independence."

Her: "Okay. Then Jamil, you'll want to fly to Washington D.C. to attend this convention."

Me: "I can't! I don't have the money. It's summer, so Amanda is off of work, and we're down to one income, and … and … and …"

Her: "What do you want, Jamil?"

Me: "A happy marriage, to lose weight, a life without stress, freedom over my time, and financial independence."

Her: "*Why* do you want these things?"

Me: "Because I deserve it. I want to be free."

Her: "Okay. Then Jamil, you're going to want to attend this training in Washington, D.C. Trust me."

Case Study Two

Me: "I can't! I don't have the time, energy, or emotional fortitude right now. Amanda and I just had the biggest fight, and … and … and …"

Her: "Uh-huhhh. What do you want?"

Me: "A happy marriage, to lose weight, a life without stress, freedom over my time, and financial independence."

Her: "Okay. Well, the best advice I can give you is to *do it anyway*."

Me: "What?"

Her: "It seems to me that what you said and did is not serving you. You'll want to apologize for that fight and the argument that you escalated with Amanda. It sounds like ego won, not love."

Me: "I don't want to apologize. I was right. I shouldn't have to apologize—it's not fair."

Her: "Okay. Well, obviously, you can do what you want, but … remind me, what do you want again?"

Me: "A happy marriage, to lose weight, a life without stress, freedom over my time, and financial independence."

Her: "Okay. Well, the best advice I can give you is to still *do it anyway*."

Me: "But …"

Case Study Three

Her: "Oh, and you'll want to save and invest the majority of your money."

Me: "But I don't want to! We've got a lot of things coming up … the kids need … I need … Amanda needs … There's a new car that looks really fly … and … and … and …"

Her: "Sounds good. Remind me what it is you *want?*"

Me: "A happy marriage, to lose weight, a life without stress, freedom over my time, and financial independence."

Her: "Okay. Well, the best advice I can give you is to still *do it anyway*."

EMOTIONS DON'T RULE YOU

Perhaps that conversation was frustrating for you to read, as we spent so much time repeating things. But maybe it's a conversation you've had before—or continue to have to this day. Ultimately, to get what you want,

They said, "When you pray, you are talking to God— but when you meditate, God talks to you."

— THINK LIFE *is* DIFFERENT

you have to realize that there is going to be some hard, unpleasant work … and you will have to stop complaining and *do it anyway.*

It's all about doing the things and making the choices that you don't want to. But you need to *do them anyway* because they are in direct relationship to obtaining your higher wants. Remember, structure over emotion. Long-term vision is way worth the short-term sacrifice.

To fully embrace that your goals don't give a damn is a true superpower. Why? Because it puts you in the driver's seat of your own life. The goal you place at the top of your hierarchy of wants desperately yearns for you to accomplish it, but it's up to you to do the work. And that's okay, superhero, because your emotions don't rule you. Whether you feel it or not, you do it anyway.

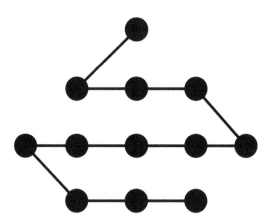

Shift Twelve

It's All a Test

"Everything can be taken from a man but one thing: the last of the human freedoms—to choose one's attitude in any given set of circumstances, to choose one's own way."

– VIKTOR FRANKL

Have you ever felt overwhelmed by past failures? Almost like you're disqualified from becoming everything you're capable of? It's a common feeling. Like watching back film after losing a football game, trying to find the moments when you messed everything up. Places we've fallen short can haunt us, and even stunt us from growing. But there is a shift that changes everything, even your past.

Our pregnancy with our daughter, Mila, was difficult. One Wednesday night, Amanda's water broke, and we panicked. She was only thirty weeks along—and it would take a miracle to make it to thirty-four. I rushed Amanda to the hospital and promised to stay by her side. But surprisingly, she sent me home, because now I had a business to run. She would take care of herself and Mila, and I would go home and take care of my duties, continuing on as if everything was normal.

Leaving my wife at the hospital didn't seem right. It was one of the hardest things I've ever done. And on the drive home, our relational issues unfolded in my head. Every one of our fights played on repeat in my head. Every slammed door echoed in my ears. Every selfish decision flashed through my mind. I was confronted by my failures. But somewhere in those moments I realized those defeats had a purpose I'd never seen.

Every situation *good or bad, hard or easy*—is more than a random occurrence. It is a test. All of our life experience is made up of tests of character, grit, attitude, mindset, love, grace, and more. Our entire beings are tested all of the time. But *not* like tests in school, where nonfailure is the only goal. These tests are the most important ones, the ones that define our futures.

Leaving Amanda at the hospital was honestly the most difficult test I had ever taken. But I finally saw that everything I'd lived through had prepared me for exactly where my family was. More importantly, who they needed me to be. Everything had been arranged to prepare me for those moments. I stood like a warrior in the arena, training through many failures to win this battle.

It's amazing what happens when this shift takes place. Suddenly, every defeat is reframed as a mentor, as a guidepost assuring you that now you understand how *not* to do it. Just as Thomas Edison had to fail with a thousand faulty light bulbs before inventing what we all take for granted today, our failures become our teachers when we accept that it's all a test. And every test is a stepping-stone to victory. And we passed it.

GROW, DON'T CONTRACT

When situations are particularly difficult or scary, like this one had been, it's easy to contract. To stop moving forward, deciding to stay put until the storm blows over. The temptation is that if we just hold our breath for long enough, the tide will roll back out, and we'll be on sturdy ground again. And then, after regaining our feet, we can keep chasing goals with everything we've got and building something so big we must find our twelve.

Don't fall for this. Grow, don't contract. Remember Shift 4: *growth equals pain*. Every test in our past has prepared us for this moment. And while I *used to* contract when things were hard, this time, I grew instead. Every trip on the path to success taught me how to put one foot in front of the other.

This is the power of a single shift. While Amanda was in the hospital, I made more calls, did more training, and provided more value than ever before—and our business actually *grew* by 20 percent during this time.

I share this shift last because it's the one that helps sustain all of the others. Understanding that every failure is still a step toward success is powerful. Suddenly, this epiphany redeemed so many years of following patterns that didn't serve me. Each test helped me learn well. I also realized during this process that I had discovered a lot about what I *still needed to learn*.

They said, "God delivers the tree, but it's up to you to build the desk."

— THINK LIFE *is* DIFFERENT

EIGHT LESSONS

Rather than being paralyzed by what I didn't know, I immediately made a list of eight things I needed to master (and fully believe) once and for all. I still keep this list with me to this day. Times like that one have taught me that getting clear on where you need to go and grow is the best way to pass any test—especially the most difficult.

Lesson One: Amanda is my equal partner.

I must value Amanda as a life partner, woman, and equal in our relationship. Because I did not think what she did was as important as what I did, I belittled her contributions. "You just sit around and watch one kid," I thought. But I internalized the truth: Amanda is my equal partner, doing work every bit as valuable as mine. We are a team.

Lesson Two: Own my mistakes.

My relationship with Amanda's family had been broken since 2011. I hadn't wanted the pregnancy. I had treated her, and them, poorly. In fact, I had not even been on speaking terms with them. I had to stand up and be honest with them. I couldn't keep ducking them and had to face that I had messed up. It was time to own my mistakes, apologize, and reconcile with them.

Lesson Three: Engaging in my family's life isn't optional.

Back then, we were already trying to find a preschool for Ezra. However, I had been absolutely absent from that process. I didn't value it—and Amanda certainly knew that. Unexpectedly, I was forced to become responsible for the search and get majorly involved. I went from moping on the sidelines to touring fourteen different preschools myself! Even though I didn't (and still don't) see traditional education as a guarantee of success, it was extremely important to Amanda. That meant it was time to make it important to me.

Lesson Four: Stay healthy in every season of life.

When Amanda was in the hospital, and I was left to myself, I buried myself in the fridge and drowned myself in wine. To be honest, I got fat! Instead of pounding food, I should've been hitting the weights. Hard times often provide excuses to fall off of the wagon. But hard times are actually when our health and best selves are needed most. This was God giving me the chance to navigate troubled waters with my own physical health even during the hard times.

Lesson Five: Grow my business endeavors even when conditions aren't "perfect."

Much like our health, growing a business requires planning, grit, and follow through. When things are hard, though, it's easy to retract. I needed to become strong enough to build a business no matter what. I've been around when "life" happens to others, and they quit. My opportunity became this question: "How can I show up *even more* during the hard seasons?" It was time to learn how to do that.

Lesson Six: Attack the day to reap the rewards of consistency.

Days don't plan themselves; plans don't execute themselves. In fact, an unplanned day will dominate you. I had to learn to attack the day rather than let each day attack me. If I failed, it was God (or the Universe) showing me I wasn't ready to take the next step. If I allowed my business to go backward, it was a sign I hadn't passed the test and would need to retake it. It was time to learn how to stop letting life sock me in the face. Every day, I had to multiply what I'd been given and reap the rewards of consistency. There is no blessing without the work, here. As Jesus said in Luke 12:48 (NIV), "From everyone who has been given much, much will be demanded; and from the one who has been entrusted with much, much more will be asked."

Lesson Six: Master my time by owning my calendar.

Without Amanda (whom I now had an increased appreciation for) by my side, I had to condense an eight-hour day into a three-hour one. I had to run a growing business, be an engaged leader, visit preschools, cook dinner for Ezra and myself, run to the hospital to visit Amanda, and complete every other life thing that needed doing. Not an easy thing to accomplish. This was especially difficult because I had never valued my calendar; I was too scared to tell people how to value my time and, therefore, was always on *other people's* time. I had to quickly learn to respect my own time to set boundaries in order for others to do the same.

Lesson Seven: Overcome the fear of saying no.

Struggling to master my own calendar was closely related to my fear of saying no. I was a "yes" man. I believed if I said *no* to anything, I was saying *no* to everything. I was scared of losing clients, business partners, and opportunities. So, I would say *yes* to everything and overextend myself. If I got invited to speak at a school, I'd cancel other plans because I was worried they wouldn't invite me back. I needed to learn the truth, which was that no can simply mean "not now." And that declining a current opportunity didn't chase away all future opportunities. The real lesson was that every *no* was actually a *yes* to what I chose to build and focus on.

Lesson Eight: Ask for help.

For some reason, it took me years to let the philosophy of finding my twelve expand into areas of life outside of my business. At this stage, I was obsessed with trying to do everything on my own. This egotistical drive meant I didn't know how to ask for help—and honestly didn't want to. I wanted to be the expert, the smartest person in the room, the man everyone applauded. Feeding my ego made me feel worthy and important. I had lived trying to be Superman, but I needed to learn that what I *truly wanted* was to be Clark Kent with Supermen all around me. I had to learn to ask for help.

I DIDN'T UNDERSTAND

Everything that has happened in my life has led to this moment for a specific reason. And today, I stand ready for new tests because of everything I have gone through before. I conquered my list of twelve things to become a top 1-percent performer in my industry. I learned how to do my own push-ups. I learned to use fear as rocket fuel. I learned to find my land of plenty. I did so because of all the things I'd learned not to do.

I had been primed and prepped by the things in my life that looked like defeats—that, until leaving Amanda at the hospital, I had only understood as losses. But there was so much more that life had in store for me, if I only learned to take it.

Today, one of my favorite things to do is reflect about all the things "they" said over the years that I didn't understand and yet still kept enough faith to do the work anyway. And now, as I write this, seeing these tests finally come to fruition, it makes me want to cry. There were so many challenges that I didn't understand in the moment that now make perfect sense.

When I was a little boy on welfare, I didn't understand.

When I was one of only four Black kids at my elementary school, I didn't understand.

When I was known as the chunky kid, I didn't understand.

When I led the area in rushing yards and touchdowns as a junior high running back, then suffered a season-ending injury, I didn't understand.

When I graduated from college with no direction, and the only jobs I could find were in sales, I didn't understand.

When we found out we were pregnant, and Amanda wanted to keep the baby, I didn't understand.

When my marriage was falling apart, I didn't understand.

When I worked hard every day and still lived paycheck-to-paycheck, I didn't understand.

When I gained lots of weight from the intense stress of my life and job, I didn't understand.

They said, "If you do all these things and more, you will live the good life."

— THINK LIFE *is* DIFFERENT

When Becky Agajanian Flammang offered me the opportunity to become a client on her health program, I didn't understand.

When they told me that, if I wanted to change my life, I should become a health coach, I laughed at them because I didn't understand.

Years later, as I look back at everything, I now understand.

It was all perfect, and as it should be.

Grateful.

CONNECT THE DOTS

The work of this shift is simple but hard: connect the dots. It is to reflect on the confusions, pains, and failures of our life and begin to trace golden threads of meaning between points in time. You see, it is only when scenes are connected that they become a story. Your life is more than a random collection of events. But until you connect the dots, the story is invisible to you.

This shift holds all of the others in place because it shows you where to go next. It shows you how to grow instead of contract. It turns you into the uncommon superhuman who is able to grow in the face of difficulty. Who doesn't settle for defeat because you know losing is impossible, as it's all a test.

About *Jamil Frazier*

Jamil Frazier is a motivational speaker, author, certified health coach, personal development coach, and the founder and CEO of Think Life Is Different, Inc. Today, his coaching network has served over 50,000 clients and is growing—but his impact didn't always look this way.

In April 2012, he hit a pivotal moment where everything was out of balance. He was physically unhealthy, financially broken, relationally poor, and mentally frayed. Simply put, he was a mess. However, after deciding to build holistic health, he found traction on the path to true wealth.

Now he dedicates his life to guide individuals and organizations to achieve financial independence, healthy minds and bodies, and thriving relationships.

If there was only one thing he could do before leaving this earth, it would be to help people everywhere learn to think well. And he's just getting started.

For bookings, email: Jamil@ThinkLifeIsDifferent.com

Connect with Jamil:

◎ | @therealjamilfrazier

🛋 | facebook.com/thinklifeisdifferent

ThinkLifeIsDifferent.com

About *Think Life Is Different, Inc.*

Q: What is Think Life Is Different?

A: Think Life Is Different (TLID) is an educational, leadership development, and training company. It's where founder and CEO Jamil Frazier and his team work with individuals and organizations to achieve their goals and maximize potential. It's also where companies hire the TLID Speakers and trainers to speak, and where the TLID books, training courses, merchandise, and apparel are sold.

Q: How did the concept come about?

A: In April 2012, Jamil experienced a massive shift, charting a course for rapid personal change and evolution. With that growth he started experiencing life in a different way, from his conversations with his wife and patience as a father, to deepened humility and empathy with business partners, to his views on spirituality, money management, and personal development.

His dress, his hygiene, his standards, his expectations, his focus, his freedoms, and his options all changed. On days where he would have been working hard in medical sales, he was now walking the beach or in yoga classes. Everything changed, and this phrase was constantly on his lips, "Man … and to think, life is so different."

While vacationing in Washington State, Jamil and his wife were leaving a beautiful home they'd rented for the week. While walking down the steps, he paused, realizing he would earn just a little less than half that day in echo income from enjoying life than he would've earned all month just years before while working fifty-plus hours per week.

At that moment, he shook his head and all he could say was, "think life is different."

Q: What is its mission?

A: To improve lives daily

Visit ThinkLifeIsDifferent.com for more ...

Made in United States
North Haven, CT
09 June 2022

20020231R00154